WORDS AND WISDOM

WORDS AND WISDOM

A Selection from the Writings of

HENRY BETT

LONDON : THE EPWORTH PRESS

THE EPWORTH PRESS
(FRANK H. CUMBERS)
25-35 City Road, London, E.C.1

MELBOURNE CAPE TOWN
NEW YORK TORONTO

Made in Great Britain
Published in 1955

SET IN MONOTYPE BEMBO AND PRINTED IN
GREAT BRITAIN BY THE CAMELOT PRESS LTD.,
LONDON AND SOUTHAMPTON

CONTENTS

INTRODUCTION

FOR many years my father regularly contributed articles on a variety of subjects to the *Methodist Recorder*, and the correspondence which he constantly received following their appearance suggested that a good deal of interest was created. He was often asked during his lifetime whether he had considered issuing a collection of these articles in book form, and since his death my sisters and I have frequently had similar inquiries.

By kind permission of the Managing Editor of the *Methodist Recorder*, Mr R. G. Burnett, and with the co-operation of The Epworth Press, whose Connexional Editor, the Rev. Dr J. Alan Kay, has kindly interested himself in the matter, the following selection of my father's articles has been put together and is offered to the many friends who have expressed a desire to have them in permanent form.

The range of subjects covered is a wide one, for (as befitted an ardent disciple of the devoted but versatile John Wesley) he was a man of many, varied and lively interests, while at the same time single-minded and unwavering in his life-long devotion to the great business of preaching the gospel. There is nothing paradoxical in this, for a real understanding of the Christian message, with its emphasis on the unique value of the human soul, inevitably generates a warm sympathy with all manner of human affairs, and indeed there is no more stupid libel on the faithful than that which would call them 'narrow-minded'.

The present volume for the most part covers the more general subjects, with a leaning towards those byways of folk-lore and word-lore which were among my father's more particular favourite studies—though, whatever the subject, the eternal verities were never far from his thoughts, and many of the articles will be found in oblique and perhaps unexpected ways to have a vital bearing on various aspects of Christian thought. I make no apology for concluding the selection with one specifically religious article, *If Christ is not Risen*, which was the very last which ever came from his pen. It had been commissioned some time in advance, for Easter, 1953, and in his anxiety to fulfil the promise made he dictated it, with the utmost difficulty, at a time when he was already seriously ill and suffering great weakness; it actually appeared in print on the day following his death. The note of robust, joyful Christian hope which it so characteristically shows—contrasting so poignantly with his extreme bodily weakness at the time it was written—made a deep impression, I know, on many who read it; and it has been a source of profound joy to my sisters and myself to know that our father was so happily able to fulfil, quite literally, Charles Wesley's hope:

Happy, if with my latest breath
I might but gasp His name;
Preach Him to all, and cry in death:
Behold, behold the Lamb!

WINGATE H. BETT

MARCH

THE month of March once had an importance that it has lost. In the early Roman calendar it was the first month of the year: it was dedicated to Mars, the god of war—hence the name. The fact that the year once began in March is the reason why we still call the last four months of the year September, October, November, and December. These names obviously mean the seventh, eighth, ninth, and tenth months. That numbering is wrong if you reckon from January, for that would make them the ninth, tenth, eleventh, and twelfth, but it is right if you reckon from March as the first month. After 153 B.C. the Consuls at Rome entered on their office in January, and so it became the first month of the year. But for centuries the legal year in England began on the 25th of March, the Festival of the Annunciation; indeed this was so until the change of style in 1752. That is why events in the early part of the year are often dated, in modern editions of seventeenth-century books, in this fashion—'20th February 1671-1672', which means, of course, that if you are counting the beginning of the year as in January it is 1672; but if you are reckoning it as from March, it is 1671.

* * *

The greatest festival of the Church that falls in March—when it does fall in this month—is Easter, but it is a movable feast. The earliest possible date on which Easter can fall is the 22nd of March. It fell on that day, it is recorded, in 1818, and that will not occur again for more than three hundred years. The latest possible date for Easter is the 25th of April. We cannot, therefore, account Easter as really belonging to this month.

But there are some interesting saints' days which occur in March, particularly those of St Patrick, the patron saint of Ireland, and St David, the patron saint of Wales. The story of

St Patrick is well known: there is some doubt about the exact date of his birth, and the precise locality where his early life was spent, but the general facts are quite certain. He was born toward the end of the fourth century, and in his sixteenth year was carried into captivity in Ireland by a band of marauders. He managed to escape from his bondage, and travelled through Britain, Gaul, and Italy. The Pope sent him to work in Ireland, and he devoted the rest of his life to the evangelization of that land. His festival is on the 17th of March.

St David was born in South Wales some time in the sixth century. There is a life of him by Giraldus Cambrensis, with a large admixture of legend. He is said to have been educated by St Paulinus, the disciple of St Germanus of Auxerre. He did much toward the evangelization of Wales, and founded the see of St David's, later called after him. A good many places in Wales incorporate his name in theirs, for Llan*daff* and Car*diff*, for example, mean the church of David and the fortress of David; and the libellous rhyme about Taffy, who was a Welshman, also makes use of the saint's name. It is a great testimony to the fame of St David that his name should not only have localized itself as a part of many place-names, but that it should have become the soubriquet of a Welshman, as Pat and Paddy have in the case of the Irishman. St David's Day is the 1st of March.

Another saint's day that recalls a great man to whom this land owes much is the festival of St Gregory the Great on the 12th of March. Gregory was a Roman patrician, born probably about the year 540. When he was still a young man he was appointed Praetor of the city of Rome. On his father's death he used most of the wealth that came to him in founding monasteries, one of which was on the site of his own home, and in this he himself became a monk. It was the age of St Benedict, and there was a great enthusiasm for the monastic life. Gregory's life as a monk was soon interrupted because the Pope sent him, as his personal representative, to Constantinople. His particular mission seems to have been to urge the Emperor to send military aid to Italy to repulse the Lombards. The Exarch at Ravenna had confessed himself unable to oppose the invaders. Gregory remained for several years at the eastern capital, and then returned to Rome and his monastery. John the Deacon, his biographer, tells the famous story of the slaves in the market-place. He saw some boys there with fair complexions and fair hair, and asked whence they were. He was told that they came from Britain, and that they were called 'Angles'. Gregory said: 'They should be called Angels. And what is the name of their province?' He was told 'Deira' (which was the territory between the Humber and the Tees). 'They shall be saved,' said Gregory, 'from the wrath of God' (*de ira Dei*). 'And what is the name of their King?' He was told 'Aella'. 'They shall learn,' said Gregory, still in his punning humour, 'to sing Alleluia!'

The result of this encounter was a great desire on the part of Gregory to undertake a mission to England. He got the Pope's permission and started on his journey, but he was recalled, and it was not until he was Pope himself that he was able to fulfil his purpose by sending Augustine, who was Prior of the monastery in Rome which Gregory had founded.

* * *

Probably the one date in March that comes first to the mind of any well-read person is that of the assassination of Julius Caesar. Shakespeare tells us that one day a soothsayer in the crowd cried, 'Caesar! Beware the Ides of March!', and when brought face to face with Caesar repeated the warning: 'Beware the Ides of March!' On the day of Caesar's death we are told that he saw the soothsayer again, and said to him, 'The Ides of March are come,' to which the augur replied: 'Ay, Caesar, but not gone.' The Ides were the middle of the Roman month and hence in March the fifteenth day. The whole of this incident, and a good deal more of the detail of the play, Shakespeare borrowed from Plutarch.

* * *

The month of March is not particularly rich in calendar customs, but there is one that has puzzled me ever since I first encountered it in the North of England a great many years ago. The fifth Sunday in Lent—Passion Sunday—was known as Carling Sunday, and it was a traditional custom to steep grey peas in water overnight, then fry them in butter, and eat them on this day. They were called 'carlings'. There was a traditional rhyme which named the succession of Sundays:

Tid, Mid, Misera,
Carling, Palm, Paste Egg Day.

The last words refer to a very general Easter custom: eggs were hard-boiled with bits of coloured rags in the water, so that they came out curiously stained. The first three names in the rhyme are a puzzle. It has been suggested that they derive from words used in the Latin liturgy, such as *Te Deum*, *Mi Deus*, *Miserere mei*, and so on, but why these should have given rise to the jingle is not at all clear. And I have never come across any satisfactory explanation of the fried peas. I wonder if the custom is still kept up.

* * *

There are a good many proverbs and proverbial sayings about the month of March. As familiar as any is the phrase about the changeable climate of the month, 'March many weathers'. Most of the other bywords relate to the drying winds of March and the drought and dust that often result, as in the saying that 'a peck of March dust is worth a king's ransom', and the rhyming proverb which says that 'March winds and April showers Bring forth May flowers'. Chaucer, it will be remembered, dates the beginning of the Pilgrimage to Canterbury from the time when 'the drought of March' had been pierced to the root by the sweet showers of April.

I think the poets have made more of March than perhaps of any other month in the year, except May and June. Most of the references to the month are allusions to the many signs of spring that come in March. Tennyson has half a dozen references of this kind in his verse. In the *Idylls of the King* Vivien's robe of samite was—

> *In colour like the satin-shining palm*
> *On sallows in the windy gleams of March,*

and in *The Gardener's Daughter* the eyes of Juliet are said to be 'darker than darkest pansies' and her hair:

> *More black than ashbuds in the front of March.*

I have read somewhere that Wordsworth was much impressed by the close observation of nature in this line. I wonder if it was some transmitted remark of his that is behind a passage in *Cranford*?

' "Wonderful man!" [said Mr Holbrook]. I did not know whether he was speaking to me or not, but I put in an assenting "wonderful", although I knew nothing about it. . . .

'He turned sharp round. "Ay! you may say 'wonderful'. Why, when I saw the review of his poems in *Blackwood*, I set off within an hour, and walked seven miles to Misselton . . . and ordered them. Now what colour are ash-buds in March?"

'Is the man going mad? thought I. He is very like Don Quixote.

' "What colour are they, I say?" repeated he vehemently.

' "I am sure I don't know, sir," said I, with the meekness of ignorance.

' "I knew you didn't. No more did I—an old fool that I am! —till this young man comes and tells me. Black as ash-buds in March. And I've lived all my life in the country; more shame for me not to know. Black: they are jet-black, madam." '

There is a stanza in *In Memoriam* which shows the same keenness of eye for the colours of birds and trees at this time of year:

When rosy plumelets tuft the larch,
And rarely pipes the mounted thrush;
Or underneath the barren bush
Flits by the sea-blue bird of March.

But the most beautiful allusion to the month in the whole of our literature is unquestionably Shakespeare's:

O Proserpina!
For the flowers now that frighted thou let'st fall
From Dis's wagon! daffodils,
That come before the swallow dares, and take
The winds of March with beauty. . . .

GUY FAWKES'S DAY

EVERYBODY knows the history of the plot connected with the name of Guy Fawkes, though he was not really the leader of the conspiracy, but he alone has lived in the popular memory. He has also contributed a word to the English language, for when we say of anyone peculiarly dressed that he is 'a perfect guy' we are remembering Guy Fawkes's name.

When James I succeeded to the English throne the Catholics hoped for toleration, but the first Parliament of the reign, in 1604, pressed for more severity against them. Some of the more fanatical Catholics thereupon devised the Gunpowder Plot. They hired some cellars beneath the House of Lords, filled them with barrels of gunpowder, and prepared to blow up the building when Parliament assembled. Some of the Catholic peers were warned by ambiguous messages, and it was in that way that the plot was discovered. After the meeting of Parliament had been postponed several times, it was finally fixed for the 5th of November. The cellars were searched before Parliament assembled, and Guy Fawkes was found there ready to fire the train. The plot had really been devised by Robert Catesby and Thomas Winter. They swore Fawkes to secrecy and then brought him into the conspiracy, along with Thomas Percy. The agreement between the plotters was sealed by a Mass which was celebrated by Gerard the Jesuit. When Fawkes was arrested, the others fled. They were besieged in a house at Holbeche, near Stourbridge, and Catesby and two others were killed; the rest were captured and executed.

Until 1859 there was a special service of thanksgiving for the 5th of November in the *Book of Common Prayer*. It was abolished, in that year, by a special ordinance of the Queen in Council, along with the services for the Martyrdom of Charles I, and for the Restoration of Charles II. An Act of Parliament was passed in 1606 which ordered that the 5th of November should be perpetually observed as a day of national thanksgiving. The Act remained in force for two centuries and a half. The popular rhyme, still used by the children when collecting for a 'guy' and a bonfire, says:

Please to remember
The Fifth of November,
Gunpowder treason and plot;
I know no reason
Why gunpowder treason
Should ever be forgot.

But it would have been forgotten in the popular mind by this time, if there had not been another factor present.

* * *

Why is the Gunpowder Plot kept in memory by bonfires and fireworks and 'guys' today, when nobody cares twopence for what happened, or did not happen, on this day more than three hundred years ago? There can be little doubt that this is one of several interesting examples where the memory of a historic event has merged with that of a prehistoric rite. Guy Fawkes and his gunpowder barrels would have lived only in the pages of history, and would have been no more prominent in the popular memory than, say, Wat Tyler or Colonel Blood, if it had not happened that there was a fire-festival dating from long before history began that was celebrated about this time of the year. There is a mass of evidence as to this which is too great even to be summarized in the briefest fashion. A few examples are quoted below, but in order to understand their significance we must remind ourselves of the conception of sympathetic magic, as folk-lorists call it. It seems very naïve to the modern mind, but it governs a good deal of savage thought, and there is no doubt that it largely dominated the mind of primitive man. Sympathetic magic means roughly that you can influence the facts of life and the processes of nature by doing something which imitates those facts and processes. It is, as Sir James Frazer has said: 'The most familiar application of the principle that like produces like.' If you want good crops of flax, with long stems, leap as high as you can in the fields when you are sowing the seed, and the stalks will grow high. If you want rain, pour out water from an elevated place, and the raindrops will fall from the sky. If you want sunshine, kindle a blazing fire, and the sun will blaze in the heavens.

Hundreds of examples of this range of magical thought and practice might be quoted. In Swabia and other parts of Germany, when the farmer was sowing hemp-seed he kept leaping up from the ground, and in Anhalt he also flung the emptied seed-basket high into the air and said: 'Grow and turn green! You have nothing else to do!' In older days in Russia, when rain was wanted, three men used to climb the fir trees of a sacred grove: one drummed on a kettle, to imitate thunder; one knocked two firebrands together and made sparks, to imitate lightning; and one sprinkled water from a vessel with a bunch of twigs. This ceremony, it was believed, would bring a thunderstorm and the desired rain. If sunshine was wanted in New Caledonia, a wizard climbed a mountain at daybreak, and at the moment of sunrise he set fire to a bundle of charms, and said: 'Sun! I do this that you may be burning hot, and eat up all the clouds in the sky!'

* * *

Now, there are a great many survivals of ritual fires in Europe that were really, in their first intention, attempts to reinforce the waning heat of the sun. These are found in three out of the four seasons of the year, but in each the purpose is manifestly the same. In the spring the sun was still weak, and needed to be strengthened; at midsummer the sun was at its strongest, but would henceforth decline in strength; in winter the sun was at its weakest, and needed all the more anything that would renew its strength. Consequently, you find fire-festivals at all these periods. But those in the winter seem to have maintained themselves best in popular usage, at least in the northern lands, partly perhaps because a fire out of doors is a more spectacular and impressive sight on a dark winter's day than on a day in summer, when the sunshine almost makes flames invisible. The winter fires in Europe were sometimes on Christmas Day or Twelfth Night and in many other instances on Hallowe'en, and it is plain that these last (within a few days of the 5th of November) simply merged into the Guy Fawkes celebration. What these ritual fires were meant to do is well illustrated by what Plutarch relates of an Egyptian rite, though he does not actually say that fire was used in the festival. He says: 'They celebrate the festival of the Sun's Walking Stick, after the autumnal equinox, signifying that he requires as it were a support and strengthening, as he grows weak both in heat and in light, and moves away from us, bending down.'

* * *

Some of the fiery rituals must have been really impressive to watch. In many parts of Germany and Switzerland a wheel, either an old cart-wheel or a wheel specially made for the purpose, was bound round with wisps of straw and tow, set alight on the crest of a hill, and rolled down. This was done here in our own land in the days of old. There is (or was within the last twenty years) an interesting survival of the rite in Scotland. A fire-wheel called the 'clavie' was burned on a hill at Burghead, Elgin, in the month of December. It was supposed to bring good luck to the fishery, but there can be no doubt as to the solar significance of it in the first instance. An interesting detail here is that in making the 'clavie' a stone hammer must be used—a plain relic of the Stone Age, of course. Another interesting detail which points to the prehistoric is that many of these ritual blazes had to be kindled by 'need-fire'—that is to say, by boring a hole in a piece of wood, and then rapidly revolving a wooden spindle in the hole until sparks appeared and some tinder could be set on fire. That was the earliest method of kindling fire known to man. There are innumerable examples from all over the world in which this primitive and laborious way of making fire has been retained in solemn and religious uses, even when easy modern methods are ready to hand. There are also relics of human sacrifice in some of these rites, and of the substitution of an effigy for the real victim. Again and again, in what is called foundation sacrifice, an animal has been killed instead of a man, as in earlier days, and there are other examples in which an effigy has taken the place of the victim. So it was in the rite of the Argei in ancient Rome, the twenty-four puppets made of straw that the Vestal Virgins flung from the Pons Sublicius into the Tiber. The 'guy' is the last dim relic of human sacrifice at some fire-festival.

* * *

We do not realize, until we have made a study of such survivals as these, the amazing tenacity of tradition—the astonishing way that rites and usages persist today, often in a rather sophisticated form, and sometimes (as here) attached to a historic name and a historic event, which really go back to the life of primitive man in prehistoric times.

THERE are some interesting examples where a legend of crime and retribution has attached itself to a particular place and person because of something peculiar about a tomb or a coat-of-arms, and one of these, at least, links up with a whole series of tales that are specially significant to the student of folk-lore. In the church at Edmundthorpe, in Leicestershire, there is an effigy of the wife of Sir Roger Smith dating from the time of the Commonwealth. It happens that there is a red vein in the alabaster which gives the appearance of a crimson wound on one of the wrists of the figure. The legend says that the lady was a witch, and after her death her spirit, in the shape of a black cat, vexed the cook at the Hall, who slashed at the spectral beast with a carving knife and cut its paw. Hence the red mark in the marble!

A more elaborate tradition has been evolved quite near to where I live. In the seventeenth century Sir Thomas Holte lived at Aston Hall, a noble Elizabethan building which is the finest architectural survival of the kind in the neighbourhood of Birmingham. In one of the windows of the church at Aston the arms of the Holte family are represented with 'the bloody hand', which is really the Ulster badge of dignity. But the local tradition was that Sir Thomas Holte was compelled to add the red hand to his coat-of-arms because in a fit of passion he had murdered the cook in the cellar of his mansion at Duddeston (where he had lived before he removed to Aston) by 'running him through with a spit', and had afterwards buried him beneath the spot where he was slain. In the year 1850 the house at Duddeston was demolished, and it is said there was much local curiosity at the time as to whether the skeleton of the murdered cook had been found beneath the spot on the floor of the cellar which tradition pointed out as the place of burial. There is no doubt that the red hand in the coat-of-arms is the source of all this.

* * *

In the chancel of the church at Cranbrook in Kent there is a tomb over which are hung the helmet, gloves, and spurs of a knight, probably some member of the Roberts family of Glassenbury. They are attributed by local tradition, however, to 'Bloody Baker', and the fact that the gloves are red no doubt has to do with the story. A chamber with iron-barred windows over the south porch is known as 'Bloody Baker's prison'. The person intended is apparently Sir John Baker, who built the mansion of Sissinghurst in the neighbourhood. He was Chancellor of the Exchequer in the reign of Queen Mary. He seems to have been a persecutor of Protestants, and especially of Anabaptists. He is said to have been killed at a place nearby called Baker's Cross, but the fact would appear to be that he died at his house in London in 1558. The legend is that Baker spent some years abroad, in consequence of a fatal duel, but on the accession of Queen Mary he thought that he might safely return, as he was a Catholic. He lived at Cranbrook in his old house, accompanied only by one foreign servant. Then strange stories got about of wild shrieks being heard from the house at night, and of people being waylaid, robbed, and murdered in the neighbouring woods. Baker continued to live a secluded life, but gradually bought back his alienated property, though he was known to have been a ruined man before he left England. Then he began to pay attentions to a young lady in the neighbourhood, who possessed, and usually wore, many valuable jewels. He often urged her to visit his house, on the ground that he had many strange things for her to see. She always refused, but one day when she was passing she took it into her head to pay him a surprise visit. Her companion, an older lady, tried to dissuade her, but in vain. They knocked at the door, but got no response, and, finding the door unlocked, they went in. At the head of the stairs there was a parrot in a cage, and the bird cried out as they passed:

Peep O! pretty lady! be not too bold,
Or your red blood will soon run cold!

They opened one of the doors, and found a chamber full of the bodies of murdered women. Then they heard a noise outside, and looking through a window, they saw Baker and his servant bringing in another dead body. Dreadfully frightened, they hid in a recess beneath the stairs. As the murderers carried the corpse upstairs, the hand of the dead woman caught in the railing, and with a savage oath Baker slashed it off, and it fell into the lap of one of the hidden ladies. As soon as the murderers were out of sight, the ladies escaped, taking with them the hand, which had a ring on one of the fingers. When they reached home they told their dreadful story, and it was resolved to invite Baker to a party, as if it were a friendly gathering, but to have officers of the law concealed ready to apprehend him. He came without suspecting anything. Then the young lady related to the company all she had seen, pretending that it was a frightful dream she had had. 'Fair lady,' said Baker, 'dreams are nothing: they are but fables.' 'They may be,' said she, 'but is this a fable?' and showed him the hand and the ring. Thereupon the constables rushed in and seized him, and the tradition says that he was burned alive, in spite of some efforts the Queen made to save him because of the religion he professed.

* * *

Now the story of Bloody Baker is precisely the folk-tale of *Mr Fox*, which is recorded by Malone, the eighteenth-century editor of Shakespeare. Malone says that he heard it from a Mr Blakeway, who said that he heard it in childhood from a great-aunt of his. When the dream is related, Mr Fox keeps saying:

It is not so, nor it was not so,
And God forbid it should be so!

Malone happily suggested that this explains Benedick's reference in *Much Ado about Nothing*, where he says: 'Like the old tale, my Lord; it is not so, nor 'twas not so, but, indeed, God forbid it should be so.'

Now, these last stories obviously belong to a type of folk-tale found in many forms and in many lands. The story of 'The Robber Bridegroom' in Grimm's *Household Tales* is another example. The outline of this story is precisely the same as that of *Mr Fox* and *Bloody Baker*, and many of the effective details are the same. In the German tale the parrot cries:

Turn back, turn back, young maiden dear,
'Tis a murderer's house you enter here—

and when the bridegroom is at the party the maiden relates what she saw in his house, but keeps repeating at intervals, 'My darling, I only dreamt this!', until the end when she says: 'And there is the finger with the ring!' Then the guests seize the bridegroom and hand him over to justice.

* * *

The classical tale of this kind is *Bluebeard*, as everyone will remember. That is a particularly interesting example, for several reasons. For one thing, it is one of the stories found, along with several other favourite nursery tales, in Perrault's book, which was the very first collection of the kind and appeared in 1697, thus antedating by more than a century the great collection of the brothers Grimm. The French tale of *Barbe Bleu* is traditional, of course. But it seems to have got curiously mixed up with both historic fact and medieval legend. The slain wives appear to have come from the Breton legend of Comor the Cursed, who married and murdered four wives in succession. But the story has also become connected with Gilles de Rais, who was the Sieur de Laval and a Marshal of France, and who seems to have had many children enticed into his castle at Champtoce on the Loire and murdered there. He was called Barbe Bleu because of his blue-black beard. He plays a considerable part in the singular history of Joan of Arc. He died at the stake at Nantes in the year 1440. Dr Margaret Murray has attempted to show that Gilles de Rais was an adherent of the old religion that survived as witchcraft in the Middle Ages, and that he regarded himself as the destined victim required by that strangely surviving superstition. I cannot think that this is convincing, though I regard Dr Murray's general thesis as abundantly proved in her two brilliant books.

Now, it will be seen that the tale of *Bluebeard* and its analogues have this in common—the plot depends upon *something forbidden*. That means that all these stories ultimately derive from the prehistoric action of taboo, still found in savage lands. Taboo may take many forms, and may relate to royalty, or sex, or food, or what not, but it is always concerned with the danger that comes of seeing a forbidden sight, or doing a forbidden deed, or discovering a forbidden secret. It is because taboo played so large a part in primitive life that the plots of so many folk-tales turn upon what is forbidden.

* * *

And it is much the same with other primitive and prehistoric beliefs and customs. They lie behind many of our folk-tales. The actual belief may have died out utterly in civilized lands, and may only survive among savage peoples, yet one is often able to trace the influence of it in popular tales and legends. Thus some talk-tales depend upon the notion (rather closely related to taboo) that it is unlucky and unwise to let a stranger know your name. Many savages today are most reluctant to tell their real names to a traveller: they may give a nickname, but not their proper name. This goes back to the fact that the mind of primitive man long ago and the mind of a savage today is unable to separate the name and the person. Your name is, as it were, a part of your personality, and therefore an enemy can do you magical harm if he knows your name. Now this is the rationale of every tale where the witch or the wizard or the ogre is discomfited by the accidental discovery of his name, like *Rumpelstiltschen* and *Tom-tit-tot*. The last story of this kind I have met with is from Sweden. It relates that when St Lawrence was building the Cathedral at Lund, he was helped by a troll, whose reward was to be the saint's eyes on the completion of the building, unless the saint could find out the name of the troll. When the cathedral was nearly finished, St Lawrence happened to hear a troll woman who was sitting on a hill outside the town soothing her crying children with the promise that Finn their father would soon be coming with gifts for them. When the troll came and demanded his reward the saint called him by his name—*Finn!*—and he was instantly turned into stone.

ST SWITHUN

ST SWITHUN'S DAY is the 15th of July, and, as everybody knows, there is a widespread belief that connects this particular saint's day with the weather. Most people would class that belief as a mere superstition, but I believe that there may be more than a modicum of truth in it. I am sure that the rational thing to do with any popular tradition or superstition is to look for the origin of it, and then we shall often find it more or less justified. It may have taken on some exaggerated or fanciful or even fabulous form, in the course of the generations, but when we get down to the essentials we shall usually find a core of fact. Otherwise the belief would never have got started at all.

St Swithun was Bishop of Winchester in the ninth century: he died in the year 862. He was buried, at his own request, on the north side of the churchyard, as the *Breviary* says, 'under the open sky, that the feet of them that came thither might pass over him, and that the rain and the dew might fall upon him'. This 'lowly wish' was a special proof of the saint's humility, for the north side of a churchyard was always unpopular, and indeed is so in some places today. There was a notion (to which Chaucer alludes in *The Friar's Tale*) that the Devil lived in the north, and this was supported by texts like Jeremiah 1[14], and 4[6], about evil coming from the north. Rather more than a hundred years after his death, St Swithun's remains were removed into the Cathedral, where they were placed in a splendid shrine.

Very little is really known about St Swithun's life. According to a biography of the eleventh century, he was a famous builder of churches, and he also built a bridge on the east side of the city of Winchester. One of the miracles attributed to him is quaint. He was watching the masons who were at work on the bridge when one of them accidentally broke some of the eggs in an old market-woman's basket, whereupon the saint miraculously restored them. After his death, many miracles of healing were attributed to his relics, and his shrine in the Cathedral became the resort of multitudes of pilgrims. The main incident in the legend of St Swithun concerns the transfer of his remains to the Cathedral. Here the records (such as they are) are very contradictory, some saying that the dead saint protested against the removal, and some that he approved and even demanded it.

The new Cathedral was built in the time of Aethelwold the Bishop. It seems to have been felt, after the fashion of those days, that the relics of some wonder-working saint were needed in the new sanctuary, to rival the fame of those of St Jesse in the older church, called the New Minster. St Swithun was buried close by, and he was already a saint with a local reputation. Who could better fill the role of the special saint of the new sanctuary? So miracles happened at his sepulchre, and it was said that there were also visions in which the saint himself, untrue to his earlier humility, demanded the translation of his remains to the new building. This was effected in 971, in the presence of King Edgar and the now aged St Dunstan. The saint's bones were laid in a shrine behind the altar, and there they were until the Reformation, when the shrine was destroyed and the relics scattered. Wulfstan the Precentor, who has left a record of the translation, says that the dead St Swithun 'protested weeping that his body ought not to be set in God's holy church amidst the splendid memorials of the ancient fathers'. This, of course, does not agree with the other story of visions of the saint suggesting the removal of his relics: but it is in character with the humility of his earlier desire as to the place of his burial. It has been suggested that this contemporary reference to St Swithun 'weeping' may have started the tradition about the rain. One form of the story is that when the appointed day came for the body of the saint to be removed into the Cathedral a heavy rain began, and continued for forty days: this being regarded as a supernatural protest against the violation of the saint's wishes regarding his sepulture. The attempt to remove the body was then given up, it is said, and a chapel built over the remains. There does not appear to be any early warrant for this particular legend.

The truth would seem to be that the transference of the saint's body to the Cathedral was accomplished without any protest, natural or supernatural. St Dunstan—the very same saint who seized the Devil's nose with his red-hot tongs—was eager to enforce the stricter monastic discipline of which St Swithun had been an earlier advocate, and was therefore predisposed to further cultus of the saint. Moreover, the Bishop, who was a friend of St Dunstan's, was actually building the Cathedral at this time, and the body of St Swithun would serve to grace the sanctuary with an important relic. One legend says that St Swithun appeared to a peasant and told him to command the Bishop to carry out the translation of his remains. At this very time some wonderful miracles happened at the saint's grave. When these were reported to King Edgar, he gave orders for the formal removal of St Swithun's body to the Cathedral, where a magnificent shrine was built to receive it. Some years later, the dedication of the Cathedral was changed. It had been dedicated to St Peter and St Paul, but now the patron saint became St Swithun.

The day of the removal of the saint's body was the 15th of July in the year 971. The story that the ceremony was marked by the beginning of forty days of rain is supposed to have given rise to the popular belief expressed in the rhyme:

St Swithun's day, if thou dost rain,
For forty days it will remain;
St Swithun's day, if thou be fair,
For forty days 'twill rain na mair.

There are several saints who are associated with the weather on the Continent in rather a similar way. One of these is St Medard, who was Bishop of Noyon in the sixth century. There is a rhyme in patois in the north of France which says:

Quan ploon per San Medar
Ploon quarante jhiours p'us tard.
(If it rains on St Medard's day
'Twill rain for forty days, they say.)

St Medard's day is the 8th of June. The legend says that once a sudden shower of rain drenched his companions, but an eagle spread her wings over St Medard, and he remained dry: hence he was called *Maître de la Pluie*, 'the master of the rain'. There is a curious connexion between this saint and a place in England. The village of Little Bytham, near Bourne in Lincolnshire, has this unique distinction. The church, which has both Saxon and Norman work in it, is dedicated to St Medard, and it is the only dedication to this saint in the whole of England. In the tympanum of a Norman doorway leading into the chancel there are rude sculptures of a man on horseback, and some birds above—the latter in allusion, probably, to the detail in the saint's legend already mentioned. Between the birds is a hole in the stone which once had a grating: it may have been intended to hold some relic of St Medard. It would be interesting to know why this village church is dedicated to so unusual a saint.

Now the belief about St Swithun and the forty days of fine weather or rainy weather has probably developed from observation of fact, though very contradictory statements are made on this issue. One authority tabulates a number of years when St Swithun's Day was fine and the subsequent period wet, and vice versa. On the other hand, it is on record that many years ago the late Mr W. C. Plenderleath investigated the weather records with reference to St Swithun's Day, and later on Mr W. H. Harding checked and corroborated his results by consulting the synoptic charts at the Meteorological Office. The conclusions amount to this. There are in the course of the year two periods, of forty days each, when the weather is more constant than at any other time, and the most marked of these periods follows St Swithun's Day. That is not to be taken too strictly, of course; it does not mean that it is rainy or fine on every day of the forty days. What it means is that for about forty days, beginning about St Swithun's Day, the weather is more steadily wet or more steadily fine than in any other period of forty days in the whole year. That fact had been observed, and all that St Swithun had to do with it is that his festival happened to fall at about the beginning of the period of forty days.

There are other parallels beside St Medard on the Continent, where in some parts St Mamertius, St Pancras, and St Gervaise are known as 'the ice saints'. Their festivals are on the 11th, 12th and 13th of May, and there is a recurrent cold spell, recognized by meteorologists, about that time. There is a closer parallel to St Swithun in Italy, relating to the 3rd of April, though there is no connexion with a particular saint. The popular rhyme says:

Terzo Aprilante, quarante di durante,

which might be rendered:

As is the third of April's weather,
'Twill be for forty days together.

I do not know whether this has been verified as having a basis of fact or not.

* * *

But I reiterate what was said before. It is never wise to dismiss a tradition or a usage or a superstition as meaningless and baseless. It would never have existed if it were merely that. There is some reason for it, which means that (however it has been elaborated or distorted) there is somewhere behind it some element of observed fact. That canon should be kept in mind by every student of the past, and it will be found that there are very many illustrations of the truth of it.

FAUST

THE legend of Faust fills the largest place in literature of all the great legends of the world, as we realize when we think of the immortal works of Marlowe and of Goethe. And it is the most recent of all those legends to take shape, for it dates from the period of the Reformation, and not, like so many of the world's legends, from the Middle Ages. There are elements in it that may go back for many centuries, but that is another matter, and would take us too far afield, at any rate on this occasion.

It would be too much to say that the legend of Faust has an historic basis, but it certainly has some links with historic fact. There was a Dr Faustus who lived in the first half of the sixteenth century, and there are contemporary references to him from about 1507 to about 1540. One of the earliest of these is in a letter of the Abbot Trithemius of Spanheim, where we read of him under the name of Georgius Sabellicus, Faustus Junior. He is described as a rascal and a braggart who boasted that he was a mighty magician, able to restore all the writings of Plato and Aristotle, if these were lost, and able to reproduce all the miracles of Christ. He was employed for a time at Kreuznach by Franz von Sickingen, the famous knight, but was dismissed for abominable vices. About this time there is a record that a Johann Faust graduated as Bachelor of Theology at Heidelberg, and this may possibly be the same man. In the next few years there are scattered references to him, as Georgius Faustus, at Erfurt and Ingolstadt and elsewhere. Manlius, a pupil of Melanchthon, says that the Reformer knew Faust, and described him in very unflattering terms as *turpissima bestia et cloaca multorum diabolorum*, and said that he had been 'carried off by the Devil some years ago'.

* * *

The legend of Faust is first found in its complete form in the *Volksbuch*, which was printed at Frankfurt in 1587, with the title *The History of Dr John Faust, the Famous Magician and Necromancer*. Only five copies are known to exist: one of these is in the British Museum. The outline of the story is as follows. Faust is a scholar who has studied almost every branch of learning, including magic. In a wood near Wittenberg he meets the Devil, who gives his name as Mephistopheles. Faust signs a compact by which he surrenders his soul to the Evil One, and in return for this he is to have wealth and pleasure of every kind for the next twenty-four years. Then follows the record of his adventures in Paris, Naples, Venice, Rome and Innsbruck: much of this is mere buffoonery. At Rome he is in the palace of the Pope, invisible, for three days, during which he plays many pranks on the Pontiff and the Cardinals. At Innsbruck, to gratify the Emperor Charles V, he calls up the shades of Alexander the Great and Roxana, his consort. He makes a stag's horns grow on the head of one of the knights, and he devours a load of hay, with the horse and the wagon. (These particular marvels Luther relates in his *Table Talk*, but he speaks of the Emperor Frederick II, and does not name the necromancer who performed the first trick, and he attributes the second exploit to a magician named Wildferer.) Among his other performances Faust produces ripe apples and grapes in the month of January, and—most famous of all his sorceries—raises Helen of Troy from the underworld to satisfy the curiosity of a party of students. Then the end approaches, and the fiend taunts him with his impending doom. Faust falls into deep misery, and expresses bitter penitence. At midnight there is a terrific storm. In the morning Faust's chamber is found bespattered with blood, and his mutilated body is on a dunghill near the house. The *Volksbuch* which contained the story outlined here was translated into English and published in 1590, and Marlowe's great tragedy appeared very soon afterward.

* * *

The legend of Faust has always had a great fascination for poets. Several German poets, including Heine, have used it, but the outstanding examples, of course, are Marlowe and Goethe. Christopher Marlowe, the greatest of the dramatists who preceded Shakespeare, was killed at the age of thirty in a tavern brawl; he was stabbed with his own dagger, which his assailant seized and used against him. His great drama, *The Tragical History of Doctor Faustus*, is the first treatment of the legend in literature, and one of the greatest tragedies in any language. It follows the legend (as given in the *Volksbuch*) in nearly all its details.

There are at least two passages in the drama that have become a part of that proverbial province of literature which is familiar to everyone except the illiterate. One is the famous apostrophe with which Faust greets the magical appearance of Helen of Troy:

> *Was this the face that launch'd a thousand ships,*
> *And burnt the topless towers of Ilium?*

The other is the poignant passage where Faust knows that the hour of doom is near:

> *The stars move still, time runs, the clock will strike*
> *The devil will come, and Faustus must be damn'd.*
> *Oh, I'll leap up to heaven!—Who pulls me down?—*
> *See where Christ's blood streams in the firmament!*
> *One drop of blood will save me: O my Christ—*
> *Rend not my heart for naming of my Christ:*
> *Yet will I call on Him: O spare me, Lucifer!*

There is another great passage which is not, perhaps, as well known as these which have been quoted: it is where Faust asks Mephistopheles, 'How comes it, then, that thou art out of hell?' and the fiend replies:

Why, this is hell, nor am I out of it.
Think'st thou that I, who saw the face of God,
And tasted the eternal joys of Heaven,
Am not tormented with ten thousand hells
In being depriv'd of everlasting bliss?

* * *

But the most remarkable treatment of the legend in literature is, of course, in Goethe's *Faust*, the greatest poem of the nineteenth century. There was a puppet-play on the theme of Faust which was popular for several generations in Germany. This was the real inspiration of Goethe's poem. He tells us that the last Christmas gift of his beloved grandmother before she died was a puppet-show, and he describes 'the imagined world of enchantment' that was thereby opened to him as a child: he was then four years of age. He saw the Faust puppet-play in his childhood at Frankfurt and again as a young man as Strasbourg. In *Dichtung und Wahrheit* he writes: 'The wonderful Faust legend of the old puppet-shows struck many and responsive chords within me. I, too, had trodden the paths of knowledge, and had early been led to see its vanity. In actual life, too, my experiences had been many, and I had returned more unsatisfied and troubled than before.' Here is the actual germ of Goethe's poem, the greatest in the literature of Germany. He had been familiar with the legend of Faust from his childhood, as we have seen. He thought out the plan of his poem as early as 1774, when he was twenty-five years of age, but he only published the first part of it in 1808, and the second part in 1831.

The first part of the poem follows the legend fairly closely, but ends with the terrible scene between Faust and Margaret in the prison where she lies awaiting death for the murder of her child. The second part has not so much to do with the legend, though the episode of Helen of Troy has a central place in it. But while there is some great poetry to be found in the second half of the poem I must confess (at the risk of being thought a Philistine) that it always strikes me as a sort of fascinating extravaganza, where emperors and astrologers, the early Greek philosophers, personifications like Want and Care and Guilt, oreads and nereids, tritons and sirens, lemures and sphinxes, gnomes and griffins, not to mention Philemon and Baucis, and the cranes of Ibycus, are all whirled together in a dizzy dance. But the end is a noble one. Faust is redeemed, for in the later years he has given himself to the service of humanity, and angels bear aloft what is immortal of him, because 'the soul that ceaselessly strives' is never beyond redemption, and the poem finishes with the *Chorus Mysticus*, which is quite untranslatable.

* * *

The last remark raises a difficult question. It is generally easy enough to translate prose, and it is not impossible to give a more or less adequate rendering of the didactic kind of verse. But one would say that it is impossible to translate the greater kind of lyrical poetry—except for the fact that it has occasionally been done! But I think it is never done except by a man of genius and in a fortunate hour. So much depends upon the measured music of the words, and often that cannot pass into another language without grievous loss. There are several English translations of Goethe's *Faust*, but they all seem to me to be very wooden in the rendering of the lyrical passages. There are only two such passages in the poem, so far as I know, that have ever been translated into English in a way that really conveys the force and the melody of the original. Thomas Carlyle was not a poet, but he had moments of poetic power, and he once rendered the speech of the Erdgeist (the Earth Spirit) into lines that really convey the spirit and the movement of that wonderful utterance:

In Being's floods, in Action's storm,
I walk and work, above, beneath,
Work and weave in endless motion!
Birth and Death,
An infinite ocean;

A seizing and giving
The fire of the Living:
'Tis thus at the roaring Loom of Time I ply,
And weave for God the Garment thou seest Him by!

Shelley was a poet, if ever there was one, and he translated a considerable part of *Faust*. His version of the song of the archangels is a wonderful exploit, for it is almost as literal as a prose rendering could be, and yet it brings to us the majesty and the music of the original. The first stanza is:

The sun-orb sings, in emulation,
Mid brother-spheres, his ancient round:
His path predestined through Creation
He ends with step of thunder-sound.
The angels from his visage splendid
Draw power, whose measure none can say;
The lofty works, uncomprehended,
Are bright as on the earliest day.

Would that Shelley had translated the whole of *Faust*, if he had done it all like that!

THE WISE MEN OF GOTHAM

SOME time ago I was being motored to an appointment in the neighbourhood of Nottingham when I happened to notice a signboard which pointed to Gotham. I remarked on this, and my host asked me if I would like to see the famous place. So it was arranged, and I paid a visit to Gotham. I found a large and apparently prosperous village, and learned that it is the headquarters of the gypsum industry in England. The largest gypsum mines in the country are in the parish. Gypsum is more important and various in its uses than I had known. It is not only a component of plaster, but it is a basis in many cosmetics, and even has a place in flour-milling, not by way of adulteration, but to give the steel rollers that grind the corn a better grip on the grain, or so I understand. But it was not for the sake of gypsum that I wanted to see the place. It was because it was the traditional home of the Wise Men of Gotham.

In every land some district has been regarded from very early times as the special home of folly: in Asia it was Phrygia, in Greece it was Boeotia, in Germany it was Swabia. Very often it has also come to pass that some particular village has possessed a special reputation for foolishness. Some of the quaintest of our English folk-sayings and folk-tales relate grotesque examples of the alleged folly of people in such places. It seems to have been a favourite form of humour in the olden days to invent such extravagances.

Of all the gibes about the foolishness of folk in a particular place the most famous example in England is the story of 'The Wise Men of Gotham'. The general form of the legend is that King John once attempted to pass through some fields belonging to the folk of the village. They thought that the royal passage would establish a right-of-way for evermore, and they forcibly prevented the King from taking that route. He was furious, and afterward sent some of his officers to punish the bold villagers. They heard of this beforehand, and thought that the best way to escape vengeance would be to pretend that they were all mad, and therefore not responsible for what they had done. Accordingly, the king's representatives, when they arrived, found some of the men of Gotham trying to drown an eel in a pail of water; others trundling their cheeses down the hill so that they would roll all the way to Nottingham by themselves; others joining hands round a bush where there was a cuckoo (or, in another version of the tale, planting a hedge round it) with the intention of securing perpetual spring by retaining the bird, and saying to it: 'Sing here all the year, and thou shalt lack neither meat nor drink!' When the cuckoo flew away they said: 'A vengeance on her! We made not our hedge high enough.' On a tumulus about a mile south of Gotham is 'The Cuckoo Bush', said to be planted on the very site where the villagers tried to imprison the bird.

Precisely the same folly is told of many other localities. Thus the people of Wiltshire call their neighbours in Somerset 'hedge-cuckoos', because they are supposed to have planted a hedge around the cuckoo to keep it from flying away. The people of Madeley-on-Severn are said to have tried to imprison the cuckoo by standing round it in a ring with clasped hands, but the bird flew away, to their great disgust; hence they are remembered as 'The Wise Men of Madeley'. The inhabitants of Borrowdale are said to have built a wall around the cuckoo, naturally with the same disappointing result. The people of Zennor in Cornwall did the same thing. So did the inhabitants of Marsden, near Huddersfield. So did 'the coves of Lorbottle' in Northumberland, and 'the carles of Austwick' in Yorkshire, and 'the fools of Risca' in Monmouth, and doubtless the same tale is told of many other places as well. In all these stories the general notion is the same. The purpose of keeping the cuckoo is, of course, to secure a permanence of fine weather.

Some versions of the Gotham legend add other follies. The villagers are said to have tried to rake the moon out of a pond where it was reflected, believing it to be made of green cheese; and to have tied a purse containing the money for their rent round the neck of a hare, and told the animal to take it to the landlord at Newark, carefully instructing the hare as to the route he should follow; and to have chained up a wheelbarrow lest it should go mad, because it had been bitten by a mad dog; and to have hauled a cow up on to the roof of a cottage to browse on the grass that grew on that thatch. Some of these incidents are mentioned in early references to the men of Gotham; some are found also occurring in other English folk-stories; and the last detail recurs perpetually in the widespread tale of 'The Three Sillies', current in many lands. Another incident sometimes found in the Gotham cycle is curiously parallel to the main *motif* of this last tale, for it turns upon trouble arising out of purely imaginary happenings. Two brothers are looking up at the sky at night. One wishes that he had as many cattle as there are stars to be seen; the other wishes that he had a pasture as large as the expanse of the sky. Then they proceed to quarrel as to these imaginary cattle feeding in this imaginary pasture, and finally kill each other in their anger.

The story of the men of Gotham is old, and there are a good many references to it in the fifteenth, sixteenth, and seventeenth centuries. Fuller wrote in 1662: 'It passeth publicly for the periphrasis of a fool, and a hundred fopperies are feigned and fathered on the town folk of Gotham.' Sixty years earlier Bishop Hall wrote in his *Satires:* 'Saint Foole's of Gotham mought thy parish be!' There is a reference in Dekker's *Guls Horn Book*, the date of which is 1609: 'If all the wise men of Gotham should lay their heads together, their jobberknowls should not be able to compare with thine.' About the same date, Coryat, in *Crambe, or Colworts Twice Sodden*, alludes to 'the wise men of Gotham who went about to drown an eel', and Wither, in *Abuses Stript and Whipt*, writes:

> *And he that tries to doe it might have bin*
> *One of the crew that hedg'd the cuckow in.*

The play of *Philotemus* in 1583 mentions 'the men of Gotham' as tying 'their rentes in a purse about a hare's necke, and bad her carrie it to their landlord'. There is a much earlier reference in the *Towneley Mysteries* (*Prima Pastorum*), where Jak Garcio says:

> *Now God gyf you ease, folys all sam,*
> *Saghe I never none so fare but the foles of Gotham.*

A familiar nursery rhyme also contains a reference, but it is almost impossible to date such jingles:

> *Three wise men of Gotham*
> *Went to sea in a bowl,*
> *And if the bowl had been stronger,*
> *My song would have been longer.*

In the reign of Henry VIII a volume of stories was published under the title, *The Merie Tales of the Mad Men of Gotham.* It was wrongly attributed to Andrew Borde, who was a famous physician of the period. (He always lives in my memory for one quaint detail. In an age when learned men had a habit of latinizing their names, he did this in a particularly ridiculous way—he called himself Andreas *Perforatus*!) These twenty stories contain only two of the incidents which are attributed to the men of Gotham in the traditional tale—namely, those about penning the cuckoo and rolling the cheeses downhill.

The villagers of Coggeshall, in Essex, had a traditional reputation for folly which comes nearest to that of Gotham. A folk-rhyme which is supposed to describe the character of several places in Essex says:

Braintree for the rich,
Bocking for the poor,
Coggleshall for the foolish town
And Kelvedon for the boor.

Many examples of the foolish doings of the people of Coggeshall are related. Thus it is said that they built a church, and forgot to make any windows, so they got some hampers, set them open in the sunshine to catch the light, shut them up, carried them into the church, and then opened them to let the light out. Then they got it into their heads that the church was in the wrong place, and decided to move it. They pulled off their coats and laid them on the ground at one end of the church, and then went to the other end to push the building along. When they thought they had moved it far enough they went back to get their coats, but they had been stolen. The Coggeshall folk, however, concluded that they had pushed the church right over their garments, and went inside the building to look for them. It is also related that they put hurdles in the river to turn the course of the stream, and that they chained up a wheelbarrow lest it should go mad, because a mad dog had bitten it. (This last, as we have seen, is one of the follies attributed to the Gotham folk.)

There must be scores of places in England that their neighbours credit with being homes of folly, and many grotesque things are related of them. Feniscowles, in Lancashire, is the place where they hang up the water to dry. At Winchcombe, in Gloucestershire, the villagers hoisted a pig on to the top of a wall that it might see a troop of soldiers march past. The people of Ebrington, in Gloucestershire, manured the base of the church steeple to make it grow higher. At Huddenham, in Buckinghamshire, they built a roof over the village pond to keep the ducks dry. At Steeple Bumstead, in Essex, they refused permission for a second windmill to be built, on the ground that there was hardly enough wind for the existing mill. And so on, endlessly!

SANTA CLAUS

THAT very interesting personage Santa Claus, according to the modern myth, rides on a sleigh drawn by reindeer, and comes down the chimney on Christmas Eve to fill the children's stockings with sweets and toys. He is really St Nicholas, and derives his title from the German form of the name, Nikolaus, familiarly shortened to Klaus. The Dutch form is almost the same, Nicolaas, and it was probably the early Dutch settlers in New York who passed on the name and the tradition of Santa Claus to the later inhabitants of the United States. Thence Santa Claus came to England. For he was not really known in this land until the middle years of the nineteenth century, though now he is an indispensable figure in our rejoicings at Christmas.

The activities of Santa Claus are all concerned with the hours immediately preceding Christmas, but in earlier days and in other lands the presents were given to the children on St Nicholas's Day, the 6th of December, or on the night before, by St Nicholas himself. This was true, with some variations, in Germany, Holland, Switzerland, and the Scandinavian countries. Thus in Germany on the vigil of the Feast of St Nicholas, some one dresses up as a Bishop and distributes to the assembled children of a family or of a school little gifts of nuts and sweets as the reward of good conduct, and gives to those who have been naughty the punishment called the *Klaubauf*. In some parts of Germany, particularly the region of the Black Forest, the visit of Santa Claus is preceded or accompanied by one from Knecht Rupprecht, a man in a frightening disguise, who knows all about the naughtinesses of the children during the year. In Norway Santa Claus has a servant called Kris Kringle: here the name is evidently corrupted from Christkindlein (the little Christ child). In the southern lands of Europe the gifts are not given to the children at Christmas, but later, at the Epiphany. In Italy it is an old woman, Befana—the name is an obvious corruption of Epiphania—who brings them. In Spain it is the Three Holy

Kings—the Wise Men from the East—who leave sweets and toys for good children at the Epiphany.

* * *

It is St Nicholas of Myra, also known as St Nicholas the Thaumaturge (the Wonder-worker)—to give him his full style and title—who is the remote original of Santa Claus, but hardly anything is really known of his life, except that tradition says he was Bishop of Myra in Lycia early in the fourth century. This is the city mentioned in Acts 27[5], where 'the centurion found a ship of Alexandria, sailing for Italy; and he put us therein'. There has been an enormous accretion of legend around the figure of St Nicholas. One of the quaintest details in the story is that he is said, from his very birth, and all the time he was being suckled, to have fasted very devoutly, every Wednesday and every Friday, taking his mother's milk only once on these days!

He is said to have been born at Patara, in Lycia, and his parents' names are given as Epiphanius and Joanna. Though a layman, he was so renowned for his piety that he was appointed Bishop of Myra. He is reputed to have been very wealthy and very charitable, giving dowries to poor maidens and helping the destitute. That interesting rhymester, Barnabe Googe, in his version of Naogeorgus, writes:

Saint Nicholas money used to give to maidens secretly,
Who, that he still may use his wonted liberality,
The mothers all their children on the eve do cause to fast,
And when they every one at night in senseless sleep are cast,
Both apples, nuts, and pears they bring, and other things beside,
As caps, and shoes, and petticoats, which secretly they hide,
And, in the morning found, they say that this Saint Nicholas brought.

St Nicholas was also the patron saint of mariners and travellers, and, oddly enough, highwaymen were called 'St Nicholas's clerks'. Shakespeare has the phrase in *Henry IV*, in the scene at the inn at Rochester, where Gadshill says of the travellers:

'Sirrah, if they meet not with Saint Nicholas's clerks, I'll give thee this neck.' The name is probably due to the fact that there has been some confusion between St Nicholas and the Nicca or Neck of the Scandinavian lands, who was a malicious spirit, and who has given us 'Old Nick' as a name for the Devil.

But the special patronage of St Nicholas was given to children, and there is a reason for this in the legend. It relates that two boys were being sent to Athens for their education, and their father told them to call at Myra on the way, and secure the blessing of the bishop. They arrived at Myra very late in the day, and did not like to call on the Bishop at that hour, so they took up their abode at an inn for the night. The landlord killed them both as they slept, for the sake of their money and baggage. Then he cut up the bodies, and put the dismembered pieces into a pickling tub with some pork. St Nicholas had a supernatural warning of this; he came round to the Inn, and taxed the host with the crime. He confessed, and begged the saint to intercede for him. St Nicholas did so, and besought the Almighty to raise the dead children to life again. So it came to pass, and the saint has ever since been the especial patron of children. It is a casual illustration of this traditional connexion of the saint with young children that the baptismal font at Winchester Cathedral is carved with scenes from the life of St Nicholas.

* * *

St Nicholas is said to have been imprisoned in the reign of Diocletian, and released under Constantine. It is very unlikely that he was present at the Council of Nicaea, but the legend says that he was, and that he boxed the ears of the heretic Arius there. The broad red face and white beard that have become the special property of Santa Claus are traditionally attributed to St Nicholas of Myra.

The supposed relics of St Nicholas were brought from the East to Bari, in the Kingdom of Naples, in May 1087. It is said that they were stolen from Myra by some Italian merchants, who planned a regular expedition to effect the theft. The stealing of relics was not at all uncommon in the Middle Ages. The anniversary of the 'translation' of the relics (to use the ecclesiastical term, which here reminds one of Ancient Pistol's choice of words) is still kept as a festival in the Russian Church. St Nicholas is, of course, the patron saint of Russia. It is odd that he should have been so popular a saint both in the East and in the West. It is said that there are four hundred churches dedicated to St Nicholas in our own land.

* * *

The quaint and interesting episode of the Boy Bishop was closely connected with St Nicholas, for he was elected on St Nicholas's Day, and held office until Innocents' Day—that is, from the 6th to the 28th of December. The whole celebration was children's festival, and undoubtedly helped to confirm St Nicholas in his role of the friend of children. The custom seems to have prevailed in most cathedrals and collegiate churches. The Boy Bishop (in the North the Barnebishop) was chosen from the choristers, and there was a proviso at York Minster that he should be a handsome lad, *corpore formosus*. He was dressed in the complete apparel of a Bishop, with mitre and crozier, and it is stated that he performed all the ceremonies in church, except Mass, during his period of office. It is recorded that in 1299 King Edward I, on his way to Scotland, allowed a Boy Bishop to say vespers before him at Heaton, then a village near Newcastle-upon-Tyne, and gave a considerable present to the boy and his attendants. This was on the 7th of December, the first day after the appointment of the Boy Bishop. This quaint business of the *Episcopus Puerorum* was suppressed by a Royal Proclamation in 1542, but restored under Mary Tudor. It does not seem to have been formally suppressed under Elizabeth, but it probably died out naturally as England became more Protestant, though there are references to the ceremony surviving in villages late in Elizabeth's reign, and it has been revived in some places in recent years.

There are a good many references extant to money spent on the Boy Bishop's robes and adornments and entertainments, like an item in the accounts of St Mary at Hill in London—in 1549 'a mitre for a Bishop at St Nicholas-tyde, garnished with silver and amelyd [enamelled] and perle and counterfeit stone'; and another item at Lambeth in 1523—'for the Bishop's dynner and hys company on St Nycolas Day, two shillings and eightpence'. It is said that the Boy Bishop at Salisbury disposed of such prebends as happened to fall vacant during his time of office, and if he died himself in that period he was given the full funeral ceremonies of a bishop, and a monument. There is, I believe, in Salisbury Cathedral, a small monument which is supposed to be that of a Boy Bishop who died during his term.

* * *

There is extant a sermon preached by a Boy Bishop, dated 1493, and printed by Wynkyn de Worde. It is evidently prepared by an adult, to be read or memorized by the preacher, but it is in character throughout, with some touches of humour, as when the Boy Bishop bids the people pray for 'our holy fader the Pope with alle the clargye, my Lorde of Caunterbury, and the ryghte reverende fader and worshipfull lorde *my broder* Bysshopp of London your dyacesan, also for *my worshypfull broder* the Deane of this cathedrall chirche'. The sermon was evidently preached in London, at St Paul's, for the preacher asks the prayers of the people for 'the soule of the reverende fader my lords Thomas Kempe late Bysshop, and for the soules of all Benefactours of thys chirche of Poules'. Thomas Kempe became Bishop of London in 1450, and died in 1489.

The first words of this sermon are: 'In the begynnynge thenne of this simple exhortacyon, that I a chylde, wantynge the habyte of connynge [knowledge] maye be dyrected by Hym that gave to that childe Danyell *Sermonem rectum et Spiritum Deorum* somewhat to say to His laude and praysynge, and to all pure chylderne that bene here present edifyenge, we shall atte this tyme devoutly make our prayers.'

STREET NAMES

THE other day I arrived in Leicester by rail, and walked to the bus station to complete my journey to Hinckley by road. On the way I passed a short street near St Nicholas's Church, and hardly believed my eyes when I looked at the name of it. But there was no doubt about it; the name was up at both ends of the little street. It was *Holy Bones*. It was, really. Fancy dating your letters from 'No. 1, Holy Bones, Leicester'! I looked it up later on in a guide-book, which stated that long ago a large quantity of bones had been discovered on the site, and these were assumed, after the fashion of the Middle Ages, to be relics of the saints. Hence the name.

* * *

This made me think about the very curious and remarkable names of streets that one encounters in different towns. There are many of these. One odd example is found in Lincoln, where I once lived for three happy years. When people talk about Lincolnshire as if it were all a dreary flat, I like to tell them that some of the steepest streets in England are in the city of Lincoln. One is Steep Hill, which leads up to the Minster, and another is a stepped ascent in the same direction which goes by the name of The Grecian Stairs. This is a particularly interesting name, because it embodies both a bit of linguistic history and a popular mistake. The original name was The Greesen, which means The Stairs. In older English *gre* and *grize* mean a step, and the plural, *grees*, *greesen*, means steps or stairs. In Acts 21[35], 'And when he came upon the *stairs*, so it was, that he was borne of the soldiers for the violence of the crowd', Wyclif's rendering is: 'And whanne Poul cam to the *grees* it bifel that he was borun of knyhtes for strengthe of the peple.' Shakespeare uses the word more than once. In *Twelfth Night*, where Viola says, 'I pity you,' and Olivia answers, 'That's a degree to love,' Viola retorts, 'No, not a *grise*, for 'tis a vulgar proof, That very oft we pity enemies.' And in *Othello* the Duke says, 'Let me speak like yourself, and lay a sentence, Which, as a *grise* or step, may help these lovers, Into your favour.' When the meaning of Greesen was forgotten in Lincoln the word was changed to the absurd Grecian, and then Stairs was added.

* * *

One of the most interesting of the street names in Stratford-on-Avon is the Rother Market. This is the cattle market, for 'rother' in old English means 'ox'. There is a passage in *Timon of Athens* where Timon says (according to the original printed reading):

> *It is the pasture lards the brother's side,*
> *The want that makes him lean.*

This was a standing difficulty to Shakespearian scholars until one of the editors—I forget which—made the happy emendation, 'the *rother's side*.' Very probably it was the Rother Market at Stratford that put it into his mind.

A street in Hull has the extraordinary name of The Land of Green Ginger. Several conjectures as to the origin and meaning of this name have been ventured. One local historian, I believe, thinks that green ginger, or something which was called by that name, used to be grown there, in an angle of the wall that surrounded the residence of the De la Poles. Oddly enough, it is recorded that at a feast given by the town of Hull to the Earl of Northumberland in the reign of Henry VI, fourpence was paid for 'a conserve of green ginger'. I have seen it stated, however, in an account of an election in 1685, that when Sir William Hickman of Gainsborough came down to Hull by the river, a coach met him at the water-side, and 'the mob pulled it right away to the George Inn at the corner of the Land of Moses Greenhinger, the boatbuilder in White Friars Gate'. If this record is reliable, the name is explained—the Land of Greenhinger is easily enough corrupted into the Land of Green Ginger. That gifted novelist, the late Winifred Holtby, took the quaint name of this street as the title of one of her books.

* * *

I do not know why it should be so, but undoubtedly Shrewsbury is the town that has the most remarkable street names of any place in England. Among them are—Murivance, Mardol, Shoplatch, Dogpole, Pride Hill, Wyle Cop, Under the Wyle, and Frankwell. Murivance is said to mean an open space before the town walls; I suppose it is from *murus* and *vanus*. Mardol was Mardevole in the fifteenth century. The word is supposed to mean 'dairy-fold,' but I do not know the etymology. Shoplatch is corrupted from Shute Place, or so it is stated. Shute is an old family name in the town. Dogpole was originally Duck Pool, I believe. Pride Hill takes its name from the Pride family, who had a residence there. It is said that Wyle may possibly be derived from a Celtic word, *wylfa*, which means a place where a watch is kept, and that significance suits the rising ground along which the street runs. Cop is frequently found in Shropshire and Staffordshire in the sense of the crest of a hill—as Mow Cop is enough to remind all who know anything of the wonderful history of the early Primitive Methodists. Frankwell is really *Frank-ville*, or 'free-town'. It was originally a settlement outside the walls of the town, and owed its existence to a desire to promote freer trade with the Welsh—trade unhampered by any regulations of the borough, which had to be observed within the walls.

The only way to make sure of the original significance of ancient street names is, of course, to refer to records of the past, and discover the form of these names in bygone days. That often gives you the original meaning. Thus there is a street in Walsall called Chuckery Fields, which seems a queer sort of name.

But manuscripts of the thirteenth century call the place Chirche-greve and Chirche-grevefeld—that is to say, 'Church-grove-field'. The ground belonged to a guild which was attached to the Parish Church at Walsall, and that explains the name.

* * *

One of the most extraordinary street names I know is in York; it is Whip-ma-whop-ma Gate, and the weird name is due to the fact that the whipping-post, where criminals were flogged, used to stand there. It should be remembered, by the way, that in our northern towns a street called a 'gate' does not imply that there was a town gate there. In York, for example, all the gates in the city wall are Bars—Bootham Bar, Monk Bar, and so on. In the names of the streets 'gate' merely means a road (the Anglo-Saxon *geat*) and so you have Micklegate for the street and Micklegate Bar for the entrance through the wall of the city. Besides this use of 'gate' as the name of streets there are two other words frequently found in northern towns, 'wynd' and 'chare', like Post House Wynd in Darlington and Pudding Chare in Newcastle. Both words mean a narrow lane, and Chare occurs very often in the older parts of Newcastle. Many years ago much bewilderment was caused to the judge and the barristers at a criminal trial in Newcastle by the statement of a witness that he had 'seen three men come out of the foot of a chare'!

Some of the historic towns are naturally rich in antiquities, but almost every town has some streets with names that are interesting for one reason or another. Though Birmingham is so largely a modern city, it has a few streets with names that go back far into the past. The Minories keeps the memory of the Franciscans, the Friars Minor, and the Bull Ring recalls the cruel sport of bull-baiting. Masshouse Lane is so called because the first Catholic Chapel to be built after the Reformation was there. Carrs Lane, which gives its name to the famous Congregational Church associated with the ministries of Dr Dale and Dr Jowitt, is said to be so called because a vehicle was kept there in the Middle Ages which conveyed the priest and the sacred elements to the homes of the dying, whence the name God's Cart Lane, which was reduced to Cart Lane and, Car Lane, and finally became Carrs Lane. Two old streets in Birmingham have the picturesque names of Digbeth and Deritend. There seems to be no certainty as to the origin and etymology of these names. Dyke-path and Duck-bath have both been suggested as the first form of Digbeth, and Deergate-end, or some derivative of *dwr*, the Celtic word for water, are conjectures as to the source of Deritend. There is still another possible origin, for Leland, the great antiquary of the time of Henry VIII, in his description of Birmingham says that he entered the town through 'a pretty street,' and then he goes on: 'This street, as I remember, is called Dirtey. In it dwell smiths and cutlers.' Has the name Deritend developed from this uncomplimentary adjective? Or was 'Dirtey' merely Leland's mistake for Deritend?

* * *

Apart from names that are odd and puzzling, there are many other street names that are interesting because they preserve little facts of social history in the past. Thus Saltergate in Chesterfield is the name of a street where the salt merchants lived—a very important class of tradesmen in medieval times, when salt meat and salt fish were the food of the people for more than half the year. Spurriergate in York keeps the memory of those who made spurs, much in demand in the olden days, when every considerable journey was taken on horseback. Pargeter Street in Walsall preserves the old name of a plasterer: it is from the Old French *parjeter*, with the notion of 'throwing' the plaster at the wall, as we still speak of 'rough-*casting*'.

Even in modern names of modern streets, selected, I suppose, by some committee or some official of the municipal corporation, there is now and again some interest. The streets around Handsworth College are scarcely as old as the College itself, but

I was always intrigued by the fact that close by there is a Richmond Road, and also a Headingley Road. It looks as if someone who had to do with the naming of those streets knew something about the location of the other colleges of our Church, but was resolved to ignore Manchester!

PORRIDGE

RECENTLY, at the breakfast table, I was challenged to write an article about porridge. The lady who dared me to do this seemed to think it was an impossible subject. But there is something interesting and informative to be said about every theme you can mention, and I imagine we may find ourselves ranging through several lands and languages and centuries before we have done with porridge!

First of all, the word has a curious and rather complex history. The Latin *porrum* means 'leek', and the Low Latin *porrata* means 'a broth made with leeks'. This became in Old French *porée*, and the word passed into Middle English, and is said to survive in some English dialects as 'porray'. Then, under the influence of the word 'pott*age*' (which originally meant anything cooked in a *pot*), 'porray' became 'porr*age*' or porridge'. The food itself is very ancient. It was called in Latin *puls*, *pultis*—which, by the way, is the source of our word 'poultice'—and Pliny states that porridge was the ordinary food of the ancient Romans. There is a reference in Juvenal which implies that in his time it was the food of the poor in Rome.

* * *

As a general breakfast dish, porridge seems to be a fairly modern introduction into this country from Scotland, but it used to be almost the staple food in the north of England. Within living memory, the weavers in Lancashire and Yorkshire subsisted mainly on porridge. Ammon Wrigley, the Lancashire dialect writer, said that in his childhood the principal food of the family was porridge, three times a day. Oats grow well in the northern regions, I believe, and were probably grown even more widely there of old. When William the Conqueror gave Holderness to

Odo, a relative of his by marriage, Odo complained that the land grew nothing but oats, and the King then gave him Bytham, in Lincolnshire, 'to feed his infant son with wheaten bread'. Probably it is the early prevalence of oats as a usual crop in the North that is the reason why oatmeal porridge has been so prominent in the diet of Scotland. Everyone will remember Dr Johnson's gibe in the *Dictionary* when he defined oats as 'the food of horses in England and men in Scotland'. Nearly half the oats grown in this island today are grown in Scotland, despite the smaller area of the country as a whole, and especially the much smaller proportion of land that can be cultivated. No doubt oats were proportionately an even larger crop in Scotland in the past.

* * *

In any case the association between porridge and the Scots is very old. I once wrote a book about Johannes Scotus Erigena, the greatest thinker of the early Middle Ages, who lived at the court of Charles the Bald. He was an Irishman—'Scot' meant 'Irish' in those days, and Ireland was known as *Scotia major*. Now, Erigena (the word means 'Irish-born') was involved in a controversy about predestination; it arose out of a treatise written by Gottschalk, the doctrine of which Erigena attacked strongly, in a fashion that would have pleased John Wesley. His book, *De Praedestinatione*, appeared in the year 851. Four years later it was condemned at the Synod of Valence and in the sixth canon of the Synod Erigena's teaching was contemptuously described as *pultes Scotorum*, 'Scots' porridge!' The phrase was not original, by the way, for St Jerome once described Coelestius, the friend of Pelagius, as *Scotorum pultibus praegravatus*, 'stuffed with Scots' porridge'. Coelestius was an Irishman, like Erigena. In very early days, therefore, porridge was regarded as a characteristic food of the northern Celts.

* * *

A curious point about the use of *pultes* and *pultibus* above is that these are plurals. Now, in Scotland and in the dialects of northern England 'porridge' and 'broth' are still treated as plurals. In Stevenson's *Kidnapped*, David's miserly uncle says: '"And, Davie, my man, if you're done with that bit parritch I could just take a sup of it myself. Ay," he continued, as soon as he had ousted me from the stool and the spoon, "*they're* fine, halesome food, *they're* grand food, parritch."' Again, in Stevenson's unfinished novel, *Weir of Hermiston*, in the early part of the book, there is a passage about the Justice-Clerk's ineffectual wife and her ill-managed household, where we read: 'When things went wrong at dinner, as they continually did, my lord would look up the table at his wife: "I think *these* broth would be better to sweem in than to sup!"' Now, the great Danish philologist, Dr Otto Jespersen, in his book on *The Philosophy of Grammar*, remarks that it is curious 'that while Southern English and Standard Danish look upon *porridge* and *grod* as singulars, the same words are in Scotland and in Jutland treated as plurals'.

When I was a boy I remember noticing country people speaking of 'a *few* broth' or '*these* porridge', as if the nouns were plurals. The usage surprised me then, but many years later I looked it up in the monumental *English Dialect Dictionary*, and found that it exists in many parts of the three kingdoms. Among the phrases Dr Wright quotes are the following: 'Will ye hev *a few* broth?'; '*These* broth are varry good'; 'A *few* broth wi' leeks in 'em.' In Dr Wright's book, *A Grammar of the Dialect of Windhill, in the West Riding of Yorkshire*—which was the author's native region—he remarks that '*porridge*, always, and *broth*, frequently, require the plural form of the verb, as in "*them* porridge weren't as good as *they* owt to 'a bin!"'

It is odd to find this use of the plural form in the Latin of the fifth century and ninth century, *pultes*, *pultibus*, exactly as the Scottish judge spoke of '*these* broth', and as a Lincolnshire or Yorkshire peasant sixty years ago spoke of 'a *few* porridge'. I do not know the explanation of this curious grammatical usage.

* * *

The importance of oats as a food in the olden days is illustrated by our word 'haversack', now used as if equivalent to 'knapsack', but the original meaning is 'oat-sack', the bag in which a soldier kept his oats. 'Haver' still survives as a name for oats in some English dialects; the German *Hafer* and the Dutch *haver*, both meaning oats, are the same word. In the Rebellion of 1745 we are told that the Highlanders began their march everyday before dawn, 'with no provisions but what they carried in the shape of oatmeal, in a long bag by their sides, which they never cooked, but merely mixed before eating with cold water'. This was known as 'crowdie'. Another word of this type is 'brose', said to be made by pouring milk or hot water on oatmeal, flavoured with butter and salt. When Andrew Fairservice says, in *Rob Roy*, 'But it's neither beef nor brose of mine', the sense is, of course, 'it is neither one thing nor the other to me.'

Porridge was not always made exclusively of oatmeal in the olden time. Frumenty, a kind of porridge which still survives in some rural parts of England as a dish at Christmas and the New Year, was made of wheat, steeped or 'creed' and then boiled up with milk, sugar, raisins, and spices. In some regions it was customary for a farmer to set aside a sack of wheat, from which frumenty was made and given to the poor on St Thomas's Day. Probably this evolved into the plum-broth and plum-porridge beloved of our ancestors. There are many references to these in our older literature. Plum-broth was a kind of beef-soup, reinforced by currants, raisins, prunes, and spices—an appalling concoction! Plum-porridge was much the same thing. In the *Spectator*, when Sir Roger de Coverley is describing the Christmas feasting at his home, he remarks that 'a rigid Dissenter, who chanced to dine at his House on Christmas Day, had been observed to eat very plentifully of his Plumb-porridge,' which gave the good knight 'great satisfaction', because it seemed to indicate a weakening of the guest's Nonconformity, of course. The Puritans and their descendants disliked the way that Christmas was kept. The plum-porridge which prevailed down to the eighteenth century developed into the Christmas plum-pudding of today by way, apparently, by the mixture becoming more solid, with more of fruit and less of meat as ingredients. I am irresistibly reminded by the spelling of 'plumb-porridge' in the *Spectator* of a characteristic joke of Charles Lamb's. He wrote to Joseph Hume in December 1807, regretfully declining an invitation to dinner, where there was to be 'a certain turkey and a contingent plumb-pudding'. He adds: 'I always spell plumb-pudding with a *b*, p–l–u–m–*b*—I think it reads fatter and more suetty.' So it does!

* * *

I must not forget the place that porridge holds in the literature of the nursery. It comes in several times where a giant or a troll challenges the hero to an eating match, with gruesome details. It plays a pleasanter part in the memorable history of *The Three Bears*, where it will be remembered 'they had each a pot for their porridge, a little pot for the Little, Small, Wee Bear; and a middle-sized pot for the Middle Bear; and a great pot for the Great, Huge Bear', and at a critical point in the story the Little, Small, Wee Bear saw that the wooden spoon was in his porridge-pot, but the porridge was all gone, whereupon he remarked, in his little, small, wee voice: 'Somebody has been at my porridge, and has eaten it all up!'

The story of *The Three Bears* is remarkable, by the way, on more than one account. First, it is a modern composition by a famous author, and the only one that I ever heard of which has practically taken its place as a folk-tale. The story was invented by Southey, but it has the genuine air of nursery tradition. As Hans Andersen often caught the very spirit of the fairy tale, so Southey once caught the very spirit of the nursery tale. Another curious fact is that a folk-element has really entered into the story, for in Southey's original version the interloper is a naughty old woman, but she has been changed into a little girl with golden locks. This is an illustration of what must have happened with folk-tales again and again; details have been added and altered by those who have told the tales from generation to generation. When many centuries are involved, it will be seen how much a folk-tale may have been changed and elaborated from the original germ.

* * *

It is odd to think that Southey's fame today depends almost wholly upon a couple of short poems, *After Blenheim* ('Why, that I cannot tell, said he, but 'twas a famous victory'), and *The Scholar* ('My days among the dead are past'), and this children's tale of *The Three Bears*. He was the Poet Laureate of his day, the friend of Coleridge and Wordsworth, an industrious writer on many subjects, and a worthy man. He was accounted in his time, and no doubt accounted himself, a considerable poet. But who today (except some scholar who is exploring the background of English literature in the first quarter of the nineteenth century) reads *Thalaba the Destroyer*, *The Curse of Kehama*, or *Madoc*, of which Scott and many other of Southey's contemporaries thought so highly? But everybody knows *The Three Bears* and their porridge-pots!

HOBSON-JOBSON

I HAVE known for a long time past that there was a book with this odd title, but I never saw it until quite recently. It is called *Hobson-Jobson, being a Glossary of Anglo-Indian Words and Phrases*, by Colonel Henry Yule. The phrase used as the title of the book has a singular history. It is recorded in its first form as long ago as 1630, in some of the earliest accounts of the English in India. It is now used in two or three senses—first of a native festival where there is wild excitement, a *tamasha*, and, second, of a word (like 'Hobson-Jobson' itself) that results from the corruption of some Oriental phrase, by way of its being assimilated to English words. It may also be used of these words collectively, in the sense of a jargon which contains such assimilated terms. It will be seen that these meanings derive naturally enough from the strange history of the phrase itself.

* * *

Hasan and Husain were the two grandsons of Mohammed who were murdered in the early struggles between the Sunni and the Shiite sects. Now, the first month of the lunar year of the Mohammedans is called Muharram, and it has given its name to a festival held at that time, which commemorates the martyrdom of these grandsons of the Prophet. It is really a festival of the Shi'ahs, but though the great majority of Moslems in India are professed Sunnis, the festival is widely observed throughout the land. The devotees go in procession, and beat their breasts and wail, '*Yā Hasan! Yā Husain!*' This cry was recorded by English merchants and travellers in various corrupt ways—in the seventeenth century, for example, as *Hoseen Gosseen*, and in the eighteenth century as *Hossein Jossen*. Finally it became *Hobson-Jobson*.

Now, this is a good example of what is called 'folk-etymology'. That is a phenomenon which occurs in every language. It is the changing of a foreign word, or a word that is strange to the populace, into something which looks more familiar. The English sailors and merchants had never heard of Hasan and Husain, but they knew the English family names of Hobson and Jobson, which sounded rather like the unfamiliar Eastern names, and so the lament became 'Hobson-Jobson'.

* * *

This kind of thing often occurs with names of places. There was a local tradition at Stanton Harcourt, the home of the Harcourt family in Oxfordshire, that long ago a fierce battle was fought there, and the chieftain rode up to an ancestor of the Harcourts, and called to him, 'Stan' to 'un, Harcourt!'—whence the name of the place! So at Andoversford, in Gloucestershire, it is said that before the bridge was built there were stepping-stones across the stream, and gentlemen used to *hand-over-the-ford* any ladies who crossed! The local explanation of the name of Teddington is *tide-end-town*, though of old the tide went much further up the Thames. I was once told by a native on the spot that the town of Haltwhistle in Northumberland got its name from the fact that when the railway was made a notice was put up telling the engine-drivers to *halt* and *whistle*! The place, of course, has had its name for centuries past; it was spelt Haltwesell in the sixteenth century, and Aldwysel long before that. At Fordingbridge, in Hampshire, which is called by the natives Fardenbridge, you are told that the place owes its name to the circumstance that when the bridge over the river was built, wages were so low that the masons worked for a 'farden' (farthing) a day! The curious name of Pennycomequick, near Falmouth (which is probably Penycumgwic, 'the head of the creek valley'), is explained by a story that Squire Pendarvis had a servant who sold his ale to sailors, and excused herself on the ground that it made the 'penny come quick'! There used to be a local legend to the effect that when the Romans saw for the first time the countryside where Exeter now stands, they exclaimed in admiration, '*Ecce terra!*' (Behold the land!), and so the later city got its name. This is hardly an ordinary case of folk-etymology, however, since it is a use of Latin, but it illustrates the same general principle of explaining by some significant phrase what otherwise seemed meaningless. It must have been obvious that the first syllable came from the name of the river, but the remainder of the city's name (which is really Exe-chester, from the Roman *castra*) would not be of any plain significance of old.

* * *

I came across an interesting example of this process when I lived in York. There was a fruiterer's near the Minster with the name 'Kettlestring' on the window. Now, I have always been interested in family names, and this one intrigued me. Usually you can make an immediate guess at the origin of a family name, if you know something about the subject. But this baffled me completely. Then one day I happened to be looking at a large-scale Ordnance map of the district around York, and I noticed (in the neighbourhood of Strensall, I think) a farmstead with the name 'Kettlestring'. That at once explained the puzzle. The family name came from the place, of course; some person who lived there centuries ago was called (say) John of Kettlestring, and so his family acquired a surname. But knowing the name to be originally a place-name was the clue also to its origin in that sense. Ketyl was a Danish name, and there was a kind of ancient tenure known as *drengage*; it was partly military and partly servile. I take it, therefore, that the name had originally been Ketylsdreng, and when the Danish name Ketyl and the old word *dreng* were no longer understood, this had changed into Kettlestring, for everybody was familiar with the kitchen utensil called a kettle, and with the twine called string.

* * *

Folk-etymology has played odd tricks with the names of many things, especially eatables, perhaps. The French name of a familiar fruit is *groseille*, the Italian name is *grossularia*, the Spanish name is *grosella*, and in English dialects it is 'groser' and 'grozet', but the *grose*, in the old form of the word 'groseberry', which meant nothing to an English peasant, was changed to the familiar 'goose', and so we have 'gooseberry'. A vegetable the name of which we have borrowed direct from the Latin, asparagus, becomes on rustic lips 'sparrow-grass', for the Latin syllables were strange, but everybody knows sparrows and grass. The name of a crustacean that we have borrowed from the French, *écrevisse*, becomes 'crayfish', for 'fish' at any rate is a familiar word. The plant that the Greeks called *glycyrrhiza*, the 'sweet root', the Romans called (by a corruption of the Greek word) *liquiritia*. This becomes in English 'liquorice', obviously because 'liquor' was a familiar English word, and 'orris' was also a familiar English word in the past, for 'orris-root' was much used as a perfume in Shakespeare's day. The vegetable that we call the Jerusalem artichoke has nothing to do with the Holy City. It was originally the *girasole* artichoke—the Italian word *girasole* means 'turning to the sun', but it conveyed nothing to the English gardener, only the sound of the word reminded him of the sound of the name Jerusalem. So we speak of 'Jordan almonds', but they really have nothing to do with the river in Palestine. In the fifteenth century they are referred to as 'jardyne almaunde', and the word merely means *garden* almond.

A very quaint example comes from north of the Tweed. There was a kind of tea-cake popular of old in Scotland, the queer name of which was 'petticoat-tails'. These are mentioned by Scott in *The Bride of Lammermoor:* 'Never had there been such making of car-cakes and sweet scones, Selkirk bannocks, cookies, and petticoat-tails—delicacies little known to the present generation.' We are told that they were thin shortbread cakes. How did they get their extraordinary name? There was a good deal of intercourse of old between Scotland and France, and many

French terms were more or less naturalized in Scottish speech. These 'little cakes' were *petits gatels* (or in modern French *petits gâteaux*) and *petits gatels* became 'petticoat-tails'.

* * *

This kind of thing always occurs when there is contact with a foreign language. Thus in the War of 1914-18 English soldiers made Ploegstert into Plugstreet, and Ypres into Wipers, for the Flemish names seemed strange and unmeaning, but 'plug' and 'street' and 'wipe' were all familiar English words. So English sailors in the past made the classical *Bellerophon* and the French *Hirondelle*—the names of warships—into the Billy Ruffian and the Iron Devil. Here is a more dignified and historic example of the same process. The word 'belfry' now means the tower of a church where the bells are hung, but the word was really nothing to do with bells. Original it was a tower of defence—in Old German *berg-frid*, 'guard-peace'. Hence the Old French *berfroi*, now *beffroi*. The association with bells has given us the form '*bel*fry'. It is odd that from the Low Latin *berefredus* (and then *batifredus*) there has come the Italian word *battifredo*, which means a watch-tower, but suggests to Italians that the word is compounded from *battere*, to beat or to strike, as if it meant the place where the bell of the clock is struck to announce the hours.

The word 'curtail' is another interesting example of this process. We get it from the Latin *curtus*, 'short', but it came into English by way of the Old French *courtald*, as 'curtal', which meant a horse with his tail docked or cut 'short'. Then it became 'curtail', clearly under the influence of the words 'cur' and 'tail', as if it meant docking a dog's tail. But the word had nothing to do with either a tail or a cur in its origin.

There was an old English word 'shamefast', which meant 'modest'. Later the ending of the word grew unfamiliar (though it is retained in 'stead*fast*') and so it became 'shame*faced*', as if it meant that shame was shown in the countenance. And there was an Anglo-Saxon word *brydguma*, but when *guma*, the word for 'man', became obsolete, it was changed into 'groom'—a familiar words, though here an inappropriate one—and so we have 'bridegroom'.

And here is a final example in a word that occurs in an old version of the English Bible. The passage in Psalm 68[6], which reads in the Revised Version, 'He bringeth out the prisoners with prosperity, but the rebellious dwell in a parched land', is, in the *Prayer Book* version, 'He bringeth the prisoners out of captivity, but letteth the *runagates* continue in scarceness'. This is an interesting word: it is the same as 'renegade', the Latin *renegatus*, one who has denied his former faith or his former allegiance. But the unfamiliar syllables of 'renegade' were made into the more suggestive word 'runagate', for everyone knew what it was to *run*, and *agate* had (and still has in some dialects) the kindred sense of 'getting going'.

TOWN AND COUNTRY

THE difference between towns-folk and country-folk dates from very early days, for as soon as a number of human dwellings were clustered together there was the beginning of a town, and in every age there must have been those who lived in the wilds, with no other dwelling near. For long ages, therefore, one of the main contrasts in the lives of men has consisted in the fact that they were either townsmen or countrymen. It is curious to think of the considerable influence this has exercised upon language. The townsman has always described the countryman in contemptuous terms, such as 'bumpkin', "clodhopper', and 'clown'. In American slang the rustic is a 'hick', or a 'hayseed', or a 'rube'—the last term, I imagine, derived from the German word for 'turnip'. But, apart from slang altogether, such a word as 'rustic', which ought to mean simply a countryman, or what belongs to the country, has acquired a secondary sense of clownishness, and 'rusticity' is now almost confined to that meaning.

The countryman has been less scornful of the townsman, or else less inventive, for I cannot recall any words which he has devised to express contempt for the urban dweller. Such words as have been mentioned above have no particular interest for the student of language. But we have some other terms that are quite interesting in their derivation. For there are many expressions of a complimentary kind that derive from words which mean a town or a townsman, and a number of others, distinctly unflattering, that derive from words which mean one who dwells in a country place, or one who is engaged in a country occupation. Some of these have a fascinating history.

The Anglo-Saxon *ceorl* meant 'man'; later it came to mean 'peasant', and then, as the countryman was always assumed to be rude and ignorant, 'churl' acquired its present meaning of an ill-tempered and ill-mannered person, and the adjective 'churlish' was derived from it, carrying the same sense. 'Boor' has a very similar history. Originally it meant a husbandman, a farmer, as in the German word *Bauer*, and the Dutch word *Boer*, familiar to us in South Africa. (We have the word, by the way, in 'neighbour', which means the *nigh-boor*, the next farmer, or the next dweller, for 'boor' seems to have had that more general sense also, which survives in the Norfolk dialect in the local use of 'bor', as when Mr Peggotty greeted David Copperfield with 'Mas'r Davy, bor!') But again it was taken for granted that the poor farmer must necessarily be rude and unmannerly, and so we speak of such a person as a 'boor', and of his behaviour as 'boorish'.

A word that has degenerated still more is 'villain'. What is the relation between a 'villa' and a 'villain'? We use the word 'villa' as the name of a superior kind of dwelling, something more than a mere cottage, and less than an actual mansion. (This particular use of the word 'villa' came to us, by the way, from Italy.) But *villa* in Latin meant an estate, or a farm, or a country house. And *villanus* in medieval Latin meant a serf who was attached to the *villa*, the farm. But once more it was presumed that a mere serf must be a dishonest rogue, and so 'villain' has come to mean a scoundrel. The French noun *vilain* also means a blackguard, and the adjective means ugly, shabby, vile.

The Latin word *civitas* means a state, a city, and citizenship; *civis* means a citizen; *civilis* means what relates to a citizen, and then affable, courteous, polite, because it was presumed that good manners belonged to the citizen, as against the countryman. Hence the significance in English of 'civil' and 'civility', which have forgotten their original relation to the city, and have come to mean simply 'polite' and 'politeness'. (There is, of course, another sense of 'civil' in our language, as opposed to 'military'. This has come about because of the natural division between the army, on the one hand, and those who were not soldiers, but merely citizens, on the other.)

This reminds me irresistibly of a good story, which has a link with our present subject. The word *pequin* originated, apparently, as French Army slang in the Napoleonic Wars. One of Napoleon's generals, Marshal Augereau, in conversation with Talleyrand, used the word, and the statesman asked what it meant. Augereau said contemptuously; 'We call all those *pequins* who are not soldiers' (*ce qui n'est pas militaire*). 'Ah!' said Talleyrand, 'as we call all those soldiers who are not *civil*' (*ce qui n'est pas civil*).

Again, take the word 'urbane', which we use in the sense of refined and courteous. It derives from *urbs*, the Latin word for a city (especially *the* city of Rome), and we still use 'urban' in reference to a city or a town: we speak of an urban district council in contrast to a rural district council, for example. But while 'urban' still maintains its original sense, 'urbane' has developed the other meaning of good manners and politeness, because these attributes were supposed to belong to the townsman, as opposed to the countryman. The Latin *urbanus* had also developed this secondary sense of courteous, but only about the time of Cicero.

One might guess that there had been a parallel development from the Greek word *polis*, city, and that this was the source of 'polite', but that is not so. We derive 'politics' and 'policy' and some other words from *polis*, naturally enough, because Greece was the home of the city-state, but our word 'polite' is from the Latin *politus*, polished, and the original sense is that of *smooth* manners, in contrast to rough behaviour.

The most striking words of this class, however, are 'heathen' and 'pagan', the first a Saxon and the second a Latin word, but they both reached their present signification by the same route. When the Christian religion was spreading in the world, and overcoming the older pagan religions everywhere, the first propaganda of the gospel was naturally in the towns, as we can see even in the books of the New Testament. It was in the towns that the masses of population were to be found, and where the

Apostles' proclamation of the gospel could only have reached dozens of people in the villages it could reach thousands in the cities. Moreover, it was in the cities that there was a higher standard of literacy and general intelligence. The first churches, therefore, were in the towns, and as the years went by it was the urban populations that became more thoroughly evangelical, while the old religions lingered in the remote places of the countryside. So 'heathen', which at first meant 'one who dwelt on the heath', an inhabitant of the remote and desolate moorlands, came to mean one who was still an idolater, a 'heathen' in the only sense in which we use the word today.

As Archbishop Trench has remarked, one hardly expects etymology in *Piers Plowman*, but the old English poet does give us the derivation of the word 'heathen'. He says of a child, that until it is 'crystened in Crystes name':

It is hethene as to heuenward, and helpelees to the soule'

(i.e. Until it is baptized the child is a heathen in regard to heavenly things, and a helpless soul) and then he adds:

Hethene is to mene after heth and untiled erthe

(i.e. *heathen* takes its meaning from *heath*, and uncultivated land).

It is the same with the word 'pagan', though there is another development to be remembered here. In Latin, *pagus* means a village, and *paganus* a villager. As in the history of the word 'heathen', from meaning simply a villager, *paganus* came to mean one who kept to the old religion when most of the world had become Christian, at least in name. It is in an edict of the Emperor Valentinian in A.D. 368 that *paganus* is first used in the sense of a non-Christian.

But, by a process that is not very clear, *paganus* also developed the sense of a civilian as opposed to a soldier. Gibbon has a note on this in *The Decline and Fall of the Roman Empire*, where he remarks that 'the meaner rustics acquired that name which has been corrupted into *peasants* in the modern languages of

Europe', and then goes on to say that 'the amazing increase of the military order introduced the necessity of a correlative term, and all the people who were not enlisted in the service of the prince were branded with the contemptuous epithet of pagans'. Then Gibbon adds that as the Christians were 'the soldiers of Christ', their adversaries, 'who refused His *sacrament*, or military oath of baptism, might deserve the metaphorical name of pagans; and this popular reproach was introduced as early as the reign of Valentinian into imperial laws and theological writings'. But Gibbon goes on to say that as 'Christianity gradually filled the cities of the Empire, the old religion, in the time of Prudentius and Crosius, retired and languished in obscure villages, and the word *pagans*, with its new signification, reverted to its primitive origin'.

What Gibbon means by his reference to 'the word that has been corrupted into *peasants* in the modern languages of Europe' is another interesting etymological byway. The word *pagus*, from meaning village, came in medieval Latin to mean a district, a canton. Then *pagensis*, the territory of a *pagus*, becomes progressively *pagesis*, *pais*, and then *pays*, the French word for country; hence *paysan*, the French word for countryman, and thence again our word 'peasant'. Once more a word that merely means countryman has acquired a contemptuous connotation, as when Orlando, in *As You Like It*, says to his brother: 'You have trained me like a *peasant*, obscuring and hiding from me all gentlemanlike qualities.'

I should like to think that 'astute' belonged to this class of words, though I fear it cannot be maintained. 'Astute' is the Latin *astutus*, from *astus*, craft, cunning. Now, *astu* in Greek means city, and the word was specially used of Athens, as the Latin *urbs* was of Rome. I think I must have met the suggestion (probably in some old writer) that the Latin *astus* derived from the Greek *astu*, with the suggestion that the city was the home of craftiness. But I cannot find any warrant for this in any modern authority.

DEGENERATE WORDS

IF a theologian were wanting more evidence of the existence of original sin, he might find it in the way that many words have degenerated, and degenerated not only in dignity, but in ethical significance. There are many examples of this, while on the other hand there are very few cases—I can only think of one at the moment—where a word has developed a better moral meaning as against a worse. 'Diffidence' used to mean distrust, and a deep distrust that was next of kin to despair—this is sufficiently illustrated by the fact that in *Pilgrim's Progress* the wife of Giant Despair is Mistress *Diffidence*. But now 'diffidence' means a modest distrust of yourself, a becoming reluctance to thrust yourself forward: to be *diffident* is the reverse of being presumptuous.

But this is an exception, and it is a melancholy reflection on human nature that words which change their meaning (as many words do in the lapse of time) nearly always change to a debased sense. A good example of this is the word 'prevent'. Originally it meant 'to go before' (*praevenire*), but it developed the sense of 'going before in order *to hinder and thwart*'. The transition in meaning is illustrated in *Paradise Lost*, where Abdiel met half-way—

> *His daring foe, at this* prevention *more*
> *Incensed.*

But the primary meaning of 'prevent' is shown in the magnificent lines from the *Ode on the Nativity:*

> *See how from far upon the eastern road*
> *The star-led wizards haste with odours sweet!*
> *Oh! run: prevent them with thy humble ode,*
> *And lay it lowly at His blessed feet.*

The first meaning of the word appears even more surprisingly when Izaak Walton records that he rose very early one morning to go fishing '*preventing* the sunrise'!

* * *

'Lewd' now means lascivious, but centuries ago it had merely the sense of 'unlearned'. A sixteenth-century catechism reminds us that in the Lord's Prayer there is nothing beyond any man's capacity to understand 'since it belongeth equally to all, and is as necessary for the lewd and the learned'. And in Chaucer's *The House of Fame* we read:

> *Aha! quod he, lo, so I can*
> Lewedly *to a* lewed *man*
> *Speke*

and a few lines before we are told that such plain and simple language is:

> *Withoute any subtiltie*
> *Of speche or great prolixitie*
> *Of termes of philosophie*
> *Of figures of poetrie*
> *Or colours of rethoricke.*

'Beastly' is a word that now means exclusively what is disgusting, but it used to have a very different significance. A beast is an animal, and 'beastly' used to be merely the adjective of 'beast' and was used of anything on the animal level as against what belonged to a higher order of life. Thus Wyclif renders 1 Corinthians 15[44]: 'It is sowen a *beestli* bodi: it shall rise a spiritual bodi.'

'Maudlin' now means a condition of tearful sentimentality generally associated with one stage of intoxication, but the word derives from Mary Magdalen (that is, Mary of Magdala), who is first mentioned in Luke 8[2]. She stood by the Cross and waited by the tomb of the Lord, weeping. It is probably the medieval pictures of the penitent Mary with tears streaming down her face that led to the present sense of 'maudlin', but what a degeneration from the name of her who had the first sight of the risen Lord!

'Proud' and 'prude' are both ultimately from a late Latin form which passed into Old French as *prud*, and which survives in *prud'homme*, a word which carries the general sense of 'expert', and also in *pruderie*, our 'prudery'. When *prud* was first naturalized in English as *prud* or *prut* it meant 'grand' or splendid'. Later it developed the subjective sense that it has today in 'proud' and 'pride'.

'Artful' originally meant the same as 'skilful', and had no sense of duplicity. In Milton's fine sonnet, *To Mr Lawrence*, he promises his guest that after a 'neat repast' they may rise—

To hear the lute well touch'd, or artful voice
Warble immortal notes and Tuscan air.

But the word 'artful' today has acquired a meaning of deceitfulness, as in the name of the 'Artful Dodger' in *Oliver Twist*.

* * *

A 'leer' today always suggests a glance with an offensive characteristic; generally it means a sly and amorous look, but it once was a perfectly innocent word that meant 'complexion'. In *As You Like It*, Colin says: 'It pleases him to call you so, but he hath a Rosalind of a better *leer* than you'. The word first of all meant the cheek. I do not know how or when the demoralization began.

The word 'cheat' has a curious history. It derives from a legal term that is concerned with property. From the Latin *ex cadere*, by way of the Old French *escheoir*, with the meaning 'to fall due', we derive our legal word *escheat*, used of property that falls to the State, or to the lord of the manor, for lack of an heir, or by forfeiture. The officials called *escheators* had to do with such lapsed property. Their manner of dealing was evidently regarded as less than honest, and so we get our word 'cheat'.

'Animosity' (through the French *animosité*, ultimately from the Latin *animus*, spirit) ought to mean 'spiritedness' or 'courage', and it did mean that at one time, but it developed a worse sense, and came to mean an animated hatred, a spirited enmity, and this has come to be its only meaning in English today. But in the seventeenth century a theological writer could refer (according to Archbishop Trench) to 'due Christian *animosity*'. 'Minion' has been adopted into English from the French *mignon*, 'darling', which is also the source of the name of the flower we call 'mignonette'. 'Minion' and *mignon* are ultimately from the Old German *minne*, 'love', which has also given a name to the Minnesingers, the equivalent in Germany of the Troubadours in France. But 'minion' has developed the despicable sense of a favourite and a flatterer, generally of royalty in past ages.

The word 'idiot' has undergone a great debasement. In Greek the *idiōtēs* was merely the private man, as distinguished from those who had some official dignity, and belonged to the ruling class. Then those who had no distinction of this kind were regarded as ignorant and boorish, and then the word came to mean intellectually deficient, as it does today. Jeremy Taylor writes: 'St Austin affirmed that the plain places of Scripture are sufficient to all laics [i.e. laymen] and all *idiots*, or private persons.' So the primary meaning survived into the seventeenth century.

'Silly' has also a history of degeneration. In Middle English it was *seely*, and meant 'happy', as in the phrase 'seely Suffolk'. It is cognate with the German *selig*, which means 'happy' or 'blessed'. Similarly, 'simple', which is from the Latin *simplex*, and originally meant 'onefold', and then 'straightforward, artless', has come to signify 'of weak intellect'.

When the word 'resent' was introduced into English—it is the French *ressentir*—it merely meant 'to feel', and there was no suggestion of hurt or angry feeling. There is a passage in Pepys's *Diary* where he reports that something that was done at the King's Council 'was mighty well *resented* and approved of'.

Dr Johnson in his *Dictionary* defined 'resent' as 'to take well or ill'. But again the worse sense has prevailed, and we never use 'resent' or 'resentment' today except with a connotation of anger.

Some words are in the very process of change today, and 'suggestive' is one of them. The word ought to mean full of suggestions, and stimulating many other thoughts besides those it actually expresses. But once more the evil sense has practically won the day, and a 'suggestive' play or a 'suggestive' novel always means one that suggests evil. Language is a great moralist, and the way that the worse sense of a word has developed and prevailed is a melancholy commentary on the evil heart of man.

EENA, MEENA, MINA, MO!

EENA, meena, mina, mo! Almost everyone must have been familiar with that euphonious formula from the days of their childhood, for numberless nursery rhymes begin with it. What follows the opening line varies enormously, according to the taste and fancy of the rhymester, to adapt Sam Weller's phrase. The fullest English version is:

Eena, meena, mina, mo,
Where do all the Frenchmen go?
To the east, to the west,
To the bonnie bird's nest.
Apples in the garden,
Fishes in the sea,
If you want a bonnie girl,
Please choose me!

The end of this shows that it is what is called a 'counting-out rhyme'—that is to say, a rhyme which is repeated to decide which children are to play on one side or the other in a game, or which child is to be 'it'. This particular rhyme was evidently known of old in Scotland, for in *The Bride of Lammermoor*, when Caleb Balderstone is talking to his master, Ravenswood says, 'But all this while, Caleb, you have never told me what became of the arms and the powder,' and Caleb answers, 'Why, as for the arms, it was just like the bairns' rhyme—

Some gaed east and some gaed west,
And some gaed to the craw's nest.'

A Devon version of the jingle runs:

Eena, meena, mona, mi,
Pasca, lora, vora, vi,
Eggs, butter, cheese, bread,
Stick, stock, stone-dead!

The commonest version in the United States is said to be:

Eena, meena, mina, mo,
Catch a nigger by his toe,
If he hollers let him go,
Eena, meena, mina, mo!

Many of the rhymes are mere gibberish with nothing of interest in them except the opening line. Thus a version from New York runs:

Eena, meena, tipsy, tee,
Olive, olly, dominee,
Lucky, lunchy, boo,
Out go you!

But other rhymes contain very interesting traces of the far-distant past. Thus in a rhyme recorded in Edinburgh there are the significant words:

Inty, tinty, tethery, methery,
Bank for over Dover, ding,
Ant, tant, tooch.
Up the Causey, down the Cross,
There stands a bonnie white horse;
It can gallop, it can trot,
It can carry the mustard pot,
One, two, three: out goes she!

And this, a very significant version, was recorded in Yorkshire:

Aina, peina, para, peddera, pimp, ithy, mithy, owera, lowera, dig, ain-a-dig, pein-a-dig, par-a-dig, pidder-a-dig, bumfit, ain-a-bumfit, pein-a-bumfit, par-a-bumfit, pedder-a-bumfit, giggy.

This, which looks so absurd, is evidently a list of numbers, as the occurrence of 'dig' for 'ten', and the mode of formation of the compounds 'ain-a-dig', etc., is enough to suggest, and there is a close connexion here with the numbers in Welsh and the other Celtic languages. The whole position can be clarified and proved by another extraordinary survival, the Shepherd's Score, to which we will recur later on.

It may surprise some readers to learn that hundreds of these 'Eena, meena, mina, mo' rhymes have been collected and printed, and it may also surprise them to be told that there are traces of the prehistoric life of man left in some of the jingles.

For example, one rhyme recorded in the neighbourhood of Yarmouth runs: 'Eena, meena, tethera, methera, pin, sithra, lithra, cothra, hothra, dic.' This is obviously a list of numbers, and there is an unmistakable relation between them and the numerals in the Celtic languages. In Welsh the first five numerals are Un, dau, tri, pedwar, pump. In Breton the numbers four, five, ten are *pevar*, *pemp*, *dek*, and in Cornish *peswere*, *pemp*, *dek*.

The Shepherd's Score is a list of numerals which has survived in use within living memory in many parts of the land, especially the north-east, and which were used in counting sheep and not for anything else. I learned them from my father, who died when I was a small boy. The version current in Lincolnshire seventy years ago ran thus: Yan, tan, tethera, pethera, pimp, sethera, lethera, hovers, covera, dik, yan-a-dik, tan-a-dik, tethera-dik, pethera-dik, bumfit, yan-a-bumfit, tan-a-bumfit, tethera-bumfit, pethera-bumfit, figgit. Now, a close examination of these extraordinary vocables reveals two suggestive facts. First, there is a trace of quinary counting, or counting by fives, for fifteen is bumfit, and yan-a-bumfit, tan-a-bumfit, tethera-bumfit, pethera-bumfit are one-and-fifteen, two-and-fifteen, three-and-fifteen, four-and-fifteen. There is a similar trace in Welsh and in all the Celtic languages: in Welsh, for example, fifteen is *pymtheg*, and sixteen to nineteen are *unarbymtheg*, *dauarbymtheg*, *triarbymtheg*, *pedwarabymtheg*. This is suggestive, for all primitive languages were quinary in their reckoning, and that is because man first learned to count on the five fingers of one hand, and it may have been long ages before he discovered that he could extend his checking to the fingers of the other hand, and so got up to ten, which became the basis of all the later systems of enumeration. I do not know anything much about mathematics, but I once asked a mathematical expert whether the number ten had any special qualification as a numerical standard. He said with emphasis: 'Certainly not: twelve would be better in every respect, for it is divisible by six, four, three and two, without fractions.' But man had only five fingers on the one hand and ten on the two hands, and so the whole science of numeration began by reckoning in fives, and went on later to reckon in tens, which was the system which finally prevailed.

Then there is an obvious relation between the numerals in the Celtic languages and the numerals in the Shepherd's Score. Compare *pedwar*, *pump*, *dig*, the Welsh numerals for four, five, ten, with pethera, pimp, dig, or the variants of these in the Shepherd's Score, and the connexion is plain. So is the link between the Eena, meena, mina, mo cycle of nursery rhymes and the Shepherd's Score if you remember that some versions of the latter begin with Ina, mina, tethera, pethera.

The explanation of all this involves one of the most fascinating examples of survival that I know. Once upon a time a Celtic language was spoken all over this island. Then came the Saxons, Romans, and the Normans, and the old language died out everywhere except in the remote and mountainous regions, where it survived in slightly different forms as Gaelic, Manx, Welsh, and Cornish. Elsewhere it was supplanted by English. But the numerals of the old language survived in a corrupted form in the Shepherd's Score because the shepherds continued to use them in counting sheep—it is said that fishermen in Cornwall used the old Cornish numbers in counting mackerel until within living memory—and the children continued to use the old numerals in playing their games: hence some of the Eena, meena, mina, mo rhymes which have kept traces like tethera, pethera, pimp in the places of three, four, and five.

It will be noted that the Shepherd's Score has been recorded as in use by shepherds within the last forty years. It is interesting also to observe that it only runs up to twenty. When the shepherd had counted twenty, he made a notch in a bit of stick that he carried for the purpose: hence our word 'score' in both senses—a mark notched or *scored* on the stick and the number twenty that it signified.

One puzzling fact remains behind all this. The numerals which survive in a corrupt state in the Shepherd's Score are Celtic numerals, and we should expect them in the dialect of the people who border on the Celtic regions. But in fact they are found where there are few traces of Celtic influence. The Shepherd's Score was recorded in the counties north of the Humber, where the population is mainly of Danish or Norse descent. How is this? The only explanation seems to be that the Celtic shepherds were left in charge of the flocks of sheep when the Northern conquerors arrived, and went on using their Celtic speech. The Norsemen were not in any sense a pastoral people, and they probably regarded the keeping of sheep as an occupation below their warlike dignity, and were content to leave it to the tribes they had conquered.

THE TERMINAL PREPOSITION

THERE is an interesting detail of English style that I once dealt with in a book many years ago that came to my mind again recently. It is the use of a preposition as the terminal word of a sentence, which the legendary schoolmaster condemned (and illustrated) when he said that 'a preposition is a very bad word to end a sentence *with*'. I think he was substantially right, but with some important qualifications. The issue was raised first of all, apparently, by one who was a great writer of prose as well as a great poet. Dryden criticized Ben Jonson's lines,

> *The waves and dens of beasts could not receive*
> *The bodies that these souls were frighted from,*

and remarked: 'The preposition at the end of the sentence, a common fault with him, and which I have but lately observed in my own writings.' (Dryden should not have written 'and which' when there was no previous 'which', though his age was not as sensitive on that point as ours has rightly become; but that is by the way.) He took this self-criticism about the position of the preposition very seriously, for when the *Essay of Dramatic Poesy*, which was written in 1668, was reissued sixteen years later, and again nine years later still, he got rid of all the terminal prepositions by inverting the order, or altogether recasting the sentence. 'The age he lived in' becomes 'the age in which he lived', 'the miserable necessity you are forced upon' becomes 'you are forced on this miserable necessity', 'people you speak of' becomes 'people of whom you speak', and so on.

* * *

In spite of Dryden's authority, and his practice, Fowler's *Modern English Usage*, generally a very sensible manual, describes it as the 'cherished superstition that prepositions must, in spite of the incurable English instinct for putting them late . . . be kept true to their name and placed before the word they govern'. Professor Potter, in *Our Language*, and Sir Ernest Gowers, in *Plain Words*, both roundly condemn the 'superstition'. In the brochure of Sir Ernest Gowers we read: 'It was, I believe, Dryden who invented the rule that prepositions must not be used to end a sentence with. No one else of importance has ever observed it, and it is now exploded. Whether a preposition should be put at the end of a sentence or before the word it governs is a matter of taste in every case, and sometimes taste will give unequivocal guidance. It is said that Sir Winston Churchill once made this marginal comment against a sentence that clumsily avoided a prepositional ending: "This is the sort of English up with which I will not put." ' Then Sir Ernest tells the story of the nurse who performed the remarkable feat of getting four prepositions in at the end of a sentence by asking her charge: 'What did you choose that book to be read to out of for?'—and he comments: 'She said what she wanted to say perfectly clearly, in words of one syllable, and what more can one ask?'

* * *

Precisely: when one is talking to a small child, but surely no one would defend such a sentence in a piece of English prose that was supposed to be carefully written, and that was intended for adults to read. There is something more to be said. For one thing, it would be worth while to ask, When is a preposition not a preposition? Or when is it not merely a preposition? In Sir Winston Churchill's sentence—deliberately constructed as an impossibly bad example, of course—the natural order would have been, 'I will not put up with', where the last word is indeed a preposition, though one that is not there in its own right, so to speak, but as part of a compound verbal phrase—'put-up-with' being equivalent to 'endure' or 'tolerate'. That makes a considerable difference. For a verbal phrase may carry a good deal of meaning and a good deal of emphasis, and therefore a preposition that forms part of it is not a little, lonely, feeble word trailing along on its own, at the end of the clause. It may carry, as part of a compound verb, a good deal of the significance of the whole sentence.

This really affects the question at issue. I think there is much to be said in support of Dryden's objection to a preposition as the final word of a sentence, but that principle is qualified by some considerations that are often lost sight of in considering this point. As we have seen, one qualification is that when the preposition is really a preposition, and is by itself, as it were, the objection to it stands good, but in many examples the preposition is really part of a kind of compounded verb, rather like that curse of the German language, the separable verb. When Bacon writes, 'Houses are built to live in, and not to look on' it is obvious that 'live-in' is equivalent to 'inhabit', and 'look-on' to 'inspect'—that is to say, the verb and the preposition together really make up the effective verb. One result of that is that the compound carries a good deal of emphasis, and that saves the situation, for it is when a final preposition is quite unemphatic that it makes a bad ending, since it leaves the end of the sentence hanging loose.

* * *

This matter of an emphatic ending is quite important as an element in style. Robert Louis Stevenson once pointed out that one of the most famous passages in literature owes a great deal of its effectiveness to the hard dentals which come at the end of the last five words. It is from Milton's *Areopagitica:* 'I cannot praise a fugitive and cloistered virtue, unexercised and unbreathed, that never sallies out and seeks her adversary, but slinks out of the race where that immortal garland is to be run for, no*t* withou*t* dus*t* an*d* hea*t*.' It is rather surprising to find how often this effect is accomplished in much the same way in our best prose. There is a striking example in the Old Testament:

'They that wait upon the Lord shall renew their strength: they shall mount up with wings as eagles; they shall run, and not be weary; they shall walk, an*d* no*t* fain*t*.' Surely everyone with an ear must realize how much of the effect of this great passage is due to the dental consonants that clinch the final words. The same effect is produced, in the same way, in one of the noblest passages that Landor ever wrote: 'There are no fields of amaranth on this side of the grave; there are no voices, O Rhodope, that are not soon mute, however tuneful: there is no name, with whatever emphasis of passionate love repeated, of which the echo is no*t* fain*t* a*t* las*t*.'

* * *

The sound of words is never to be forgotten or neglected in the study of English style, either the sound of a single word, or the complex of sounds in a sentence. The part that is played by alliteration in our poetry and our prose is enough to teach us that. And by alliteration I do not merely mean the obvious kind that is satirized in the phrase about 'alliteration's artful aid', but the subtle harmonies of sound that are heard in any great passage of prose or poetry. Take as one example the first that comes to my mind: the opening lines of Shakespeare's wonderful description of the barge of Cleopatra:

> *The barge she sat in, like a burnish'd throne,*
> *Burn'd on the water: the poop was beaten gold;*
> *Purple the sails, and so perfumed that*
> *The winds were love-sick with them.*

There is no alliteration here of the patent and prominent kind, where several successive words begin with the same letter, but consider how much of the remarkable harmony of the passage depends upon a sort of verbal symphony in B.R. and P.R.—barge . . . burnished . . . burned . . . poop . . . purple . . . perfumed.

* * *

It seems to me that critics who dismiss so cavalierly Dryden's objection to the preposition at the end of the sentence forget (as other critics do on other occasions) the element of sound. They argue the matter as if it were merely a matter of grammar, or at most of expression. They ignore the fact that language is first and last speech. The spoken word was before the written word. Writing is merely a device which represents to the eye the sound of the words and therefore suggests the meaning of the words without employing the ear. But we never ought to forget that the word is first of all a sound, and that even when we are reading silently we do hear the sound of the words as a sort of undertone in our minds. Sound is never out of the question in language, most of all when any delicate question of style arises. And the objection to a preposition at the end of a sentence, in so far as it is justified at all, is justified on the score of sound in relation to terminal emphasis.

* * *

The most important parts of a sentence are the beginning and the end of it. If you have a striking beginning and a memorable end, especially the latter, the interior of the sentence can almost take care of itself. It is recorded that Gautier once exclaimed: 'What do you think Flaubert said to me the other day? "It is finished. I have another ten pages to write, but I have all my phrase-endings"' (*mes chutes de phrases*). The method seems fantastic, but there is something in it. For nearly every memorable passage in literature will be found, upon analysis, to owe a good deal to the way it ends, in respect of sound. Now it is not often that a memorable climax can be brought about at the end of a clause or a sentence when the last word is a mere preposition. That is the real reason for the axiom that a preposition is a bad word to end a sentence *with*. It *is*, as a rule—though there are exceptions, as we have seen—because it is not generally in itself a resounding, emphatic word that gives the end a sound of finality.

PUNS

WHAT is the derivation of the word *pun*? There is some obscurity about it. The word seems to have come into use in the seventeenth century as a shortened form of *punnet* or *pundigrion*, words which meant the same thing, but had become obsolete. It may be derived from the Italian *puntiglio*, 'a fine point', which had been previously used of a verbal quibble. Oddly enough, the French word for 'pun' (*calembour*) is of unknown derivation.

A pun has been often described as the lowest form of wit. That is hardly fair, I think. A really good pun has the very essence of wit in it. For what is wit essentially? In the sense of Hobbes's 'sudden glory', it is the instant perception of some incongruous likeness between unlike things—the likeness in the case of a pun being in the sameness of the word, and the unlikeness in the different senses which the word is made to carry. It is only the witty mind that discerns this double sense: the stupid do not see it, as in the eighteenth-century riddle, 'Why was the elephant the last to get into the Ark?' 'Because he had to pack his trunk!' which someone repeated as a good joke that he had heard, but he made the answer to the riddle: 'Because he had to pack his portmanteau!'

It is rather surprising to find in classical treatises on style, like Aristotle's *Rhetoric* and Cicero's *Orators and Oratory*, considerable sections dealing with puns. But this did not mean precisely what we mean when we speak of puns. The element of humour is altogether absent, and the concern of these authorities is merely with the use of the same word in different senses, which they seem to have regarded as a very effective device in rhetoric and oratory. Aristotle, for example, quotes an orator as saying that 'the sovereignty [*arche*] of the sea was not the beginning [*arche*] of evils to the Athenians, since it was a gain to them'—the word *arche* having the sense both of 'sovereignty' and 'the beginning'. This would seem to us today rather a thing to be avoided, and in any case a triviality, but never an ornament of literary or oratorical style.

Oliver Wendell Holmes, in *The Autocrat of the Breakfast Table*, has a characteristic passage on puns in which he quotes a double-barrelled one of Queen Elizabeth. 'Ye be *burly*, my Lord of Burleigh,' she remarked to her faithful servant, 'but ye shall make *less stir* in our realm than my Lord of Leicester.' The *Autocrat* adds a couple more of the same period. Lord Bacon playfully declared himself 'a descendant of '*Og*, the King of Bashan'. And Sir Philip Sidney jested in his last moments with the soldier who had brought him water in a helmet on wasting a *casque full* on a dying man. It was the habit of the age. In the seventeenth century everybody did it. The bishops punned in the pulpit, the judges punned on the bench, and the man of letters punned (often atrociously) in what he wrote, of which Shakespeare is a sufficient example. To the mind of today puns in the pulpit seem irreverent and improper, except when the pun is redeemed by a quaint sense of devotion, as when Fuller described the Holy Innocents as '*the infantry* of the noble army of martyrs'. The fondness for punning in the seventeenth century always seems to be connected, in my mind at least, with the prevalent passion for emblems, and anagrams, and poems printed in the shape of a butterfly, and the other 'conceits' that were fashionable at the time. I wonder where the connexion (if there is one) really lies? It will be news to some people that there are puns to be found in the Bible. The best example, to my mind, is that in Jeremiah 1[11]: 'The word of the Lord came unto me, saying, Jeremiah, what seest thou? and I said, I see a rod of an almond tree. Then said the Lord unto me, Thou hast well seen, for I watch over my word to perform it.' Now, the Hebrew word for almond, *shaked*, means 'the watcher', because it is the first tree to wake to life after the winter. Thus in the passage quoted we have '*the almond tree'*, *shaked*, and '*I will watch'*, *shoked*, from the same root. The almond is used as the emblem of the divine forwardness in bringing the promises of God to fulfilment.

There are some famous puns associated with the evangelization of England under Pope Gregory the Great in the sixth century. Gregory was a really great man. It is not an accident that there are only two Popes who are called both 'Saint' and 'the Great', Gregory and Leo. Everybody knows the story of Gregory's punning replies in the slave-market at Rome. Gregory must have been an inveterate punster, for there is another story about him (and there is no reason to doubt the authenticity of it, so far as I know) which involves a pun. After the incident in the slave-market it is related that he went to the Pope and begged his permission to go to Britain as a missionary. The Pope gave a reluctant consent, for which he was bitterly abused by the populace of Rome, and Gregory set out secretly, accompanied by some of his monks. On the third day afterward, on their way to the coast, they were resting awhile at midday, and Gregory was reading, when a locust settled on his book. He evidently took this for an omen, for he showed it to his companions and said: '*Locusta* signifies *loco sta*—stay where you are.' While he spoke, messengers from the Pope arrived on horseback bearing an urgent recall.

But when, shortly afterward, Gregory became Pope himself he did not forget his desire for the evangelization of Britain, and he sent hither Augustine and his companions.

The only time I ever visited Rome, nearly forty years ago, I made a pilgrimage to one spot that ought to be sacred to every Englishman—the Church of St Gregory the Great. It was on this spot that Augustine said farewell to Gregory. Here, kneeling on the greensward, the first missionaries to Kent received a parting blessing from the great Pontiff. The Church of San Gregorio only dates from the eighteenth century: it was rebuilt in 1734 by Francesco Ferrari. But the site is the actual site of the house in which Gregory dwelt, and which he turned into a monastery.

The very best pun I know is in Italian, and it is memorable also because it administered a deserved rebuke to Napoleon at the height of his power. Bonaparte was in Italy, and had been robbing the churches and the museums to send their art treasures to Paris. He was talking to an Italian countess (it should be remembered that he was often reckoned an Italian himself), and when something had piqued him he said rudely: 'All Italians are thieves' ('*Tutti Italiani sono ladrone*'). The lady instantly replied: '*Non tutti, Altesse, ma buona parte*' ('*Not all*, your Highness, but *a good part*'). Napoleon could not miss the implication, for *buona parte* might be taken either in the sense of 'a good part', or in the sense of *Bonaparte*, and he could not be offended, for the innocent meaning was there on the surface!

The mention of Napoleon reminds me of a famous pun associated with the name of a great military commander, Sir Charles James Napier. During the Indian Mutiny, when Scinde was captured after terrific fighting, Napier sent off the laconic despatch *Peccavi!* (the Latin word that means 'I have sinned!') read, as it was meant to be: '*I have Scinde!*'

* * *

Reverting to the literary writers, we may note that both Dr Johnson and Addison and Steele of the *Spectator* expressed a contempt for puns. But Boswell could not help airing one of his own, which won a laugh from his hero. 'I have mentioned Johnson's general aversion to puns. He once, however, endured one of mine. When we were talking of a numerous company in which he had distinguished himself highly, I said: "Sir, you were a cod surrounded by smelts. Is not this enough for you at a time when you were not fishing for compliments?" He laughed at this with a complacent approbation.' And poor as the pun was and awkward as the compliment was, doubtless Boswell went to his lodging much exalted by the 'complacent approbation' of the man who was his demi-god.

Addison in the *Spectator* condemns as a fault in Milton's style that he often affects a kind of pun in his works, as in these passages:

> *And brought into the* world *a* world *of woe . . .*

and:

> *Begirt th' Almighty throne*
> Beseeching *or* besieging.

Today we should think of such examples as mere assonances, but in the eighteenth century, as in classical times, they were apparently classed as puns.

LITERARY BLUNDERS

THIS is a world where blunders abound, and there are many species of them. A curious chapter might be compiled on the subject of literary errors, especially those in poetry and in fiction. The whole question of factual accuracy in imaginative writing is rather an interesting issue. Shakespeare introduces a striking clock into *Julius Caesar*. Brutus says, 'Peace! count the clock,' and Cassius answers: 'The clock hath stricken three.' But clocks that strike the hour were not invented until more than a thousand years after the time of Caesar. And in *The Winter's Tale* Shakespeare gives Bohemia a sea-coast. Antigonus says, 'Then our ship hath touch'd upon The deserts of Bohemia?' and the sailor answers: 'Ay, my lord, and fear We have landed in ill time: the skies look grimly.' But Bohemia is a land-locked country, as everybody knows. Shakespeare was careless in many things, and his age was probably not very sensitive to accuracy of detail. Our time is certainly far more so, and naturally the question arises most of all in historical fiction. There is no difficulty, or there should be none, about being true to fact in the details of contemporary life, but a historical novel, as an account of life in a past age, should fit accurately into the framework of historical facts, and it is not always easy to make it do that, unless you know your period very well. The same applies to the dialogue. The author should make his characters talk as men did talk in that particular age, or his educated readers will get some shocks. I once reviewed a novel which professed to be a tale of the seventeenth-century, and one of the characters referred to the 'scientists' of that age. That nearly ruined the book for me. Anyone in that century would have described those we call scientists as 'natural philosophers'. The word 'scientist' did not appear in the English language until the year 1840.

* * *

The Cloister and the Hearth is not only one of the very greatest of all historical novels, but it is certainly the most accurate of them all in historic details. This is largely due to Charles Reade's method of laborious compilation from genuine authorities. Anyone who has ever 'tracked his footsteps in the snow' (to use Dryden's phrase) knows how he used Erasmus, Coryate, Fynes Moryson, and Montaigne as sources of accurate detail. He was a pioneer, in fact, in this species of realism, and he could have given documentary warrant for almost all that he relates in the book. Yet there are at least two points where he has gone wrong. One is where he lets Gerard use phosphorus to make the dead robber terrifying to his comrades during the fight at the inn—one of the greatest scenes in the story. Phosphorus was only discovered in 1669 by Brandt, an alchemist who lived at Hamburg, and the time of the novel is about 1455-65, so that the knowledge of phosphorus is antedated by a couple of centuries.

There is another anachronism in the book that is more serious. When Pope Pius II is talking to Fra Colonna and Jacques Bonaventura in the Vatican Library, he says that the Friar is 'far more a heretic than Huss, whom I saw burned with these eyes, and oh! he died like a martyr'. Now, the Pope was born in 1405, and Huss was burned at Constance in 1415, and there is not the slightest likelihood that the ten-year-old boy from the neighbourhood of Siena was present at the martyrdom. It is evident that Reade has confused the Council of Constance, where the Bohemian reformer perished, with the later Council of Basle, at which Aeneas Sylvius Piccolomini was present, and where he was quite a prominent personage. He became Pope in 1458, and he owed his advancement largely to the kind of prominence that he attained in the ecclesiastical politics that were associated with the Council of Basle; but it is all but impossible that he should have been present at Constance as a boy.

* * *

But all the mistakes in historical novels are not historical mistakes.

One of the classical blunders in fiction is in *The Antiquary*, where Scott makes the sun set in the east. When Sir Arthur Wardour and his daughter Isabella were walking home from Monkbarns to Knockwinnock by the sands we read that 'the sun was now resting his huge disk upon the edge of the level ocean, and gilded the accumulation of towering clouds through which he had travelled the livelong day, and which now assembled on all sides, like misfortunes and disasters round a sinking empire and falling monarch'. Now we are told at the very beginning of the novel that Monkbarns, the residence of Mr Oldbuck, was 'in the neighbourhood of a thriving seaport town on the north-eastern coast of Scotland', which Scott calls Fairport, and which is supposed to be more or less identified with Arbroath. The cliffs at Red Head in the neighbourhood of that town are said to be the scene of the incident in the novel, for here, as everywhere else, there is a popular passion for identifying the famous scenes of fiction with actual places. It is probable enough, of course, that Scott had this particular piece of coast in mind when he wrote the tale.

Stevenson commented on this blunder of Scott's in the delightful essay entitled *My First Book*, where he says that he himself 'came to grief over the moon in *Prince Otto*, and as soon as that was pointed out to me, adopted a precaution which I recommend to other men—I never write now without an almanack'. He recommended also a map of the country, and a plan of every house in which the action of a tale takes place. 'With the map before him, he will scarce allow the sun to set in the east, as it does in *The Antiquary*. With the almanack at hand, he will scarce allow two horsemen, journeying on the most urgent affair, to employ six days, from three of the Monday morning till late in the Saturday night, upon a journey of, say, ninety or a hundred miles, and before the week is out, and still on the same nags, to cover fifty in one day, as may be read at length in the inimitable novel of *Rob Roy*.'

*　　　　*　　　　*

There is an extraordinary slip in one of Stevenson's own books. He was generally careful in details, but in *The Master of Ballantrae* there is one thing which he somewhere acknowledges as a *bêtise*, though I cannot lay my finger on the passage in which he says this—it is in one of his letters, I think. After the duel, when the wife of Henry Durie went with Mackellar to the place where the brothers had fought, we read that 'she spied the sword, picked it up, and seeing the blood, let it fall again with her hands thrown wide. "Ah!" she cried. And then, with an instant courage, handled it the second time, and thrust it to the hilt into the frozen ground.' The strongest of men could not have done that, let alone the frail arm of a woman. The detail is an effective one—a really dramatic touch—but unfortunately it is a physical impossibility.

* * *

Those of us who are old enough remember the furore created in the *Strand Magazine* by the Sherlock Holmes stories, when crowds besieged the bookstalls at the beginning of every month, eager for the new adventure of the famous detective. Conan Doyle did not think highly of these stories—he always wanted his fame to rest upon his historical novels, *The White Company* and the rest. Perhaps that is why he was sometimes extremely careless about his details in the detective stories. The most obvious blunder relates to Dr Watson's wound. It will be remembered that he is said to have been an Assistant Surgeon in the Army and to have been through the Second Afghan War. He says in his own account of his career: 'I was attached to the Berkshires, with whom I served at the fatal Battle of Maiwand. There I was struck on the shoulder by a Jezail bullet which shattered the bone and grazed the subclavian artery.' This is at the beginning of *A Study in Scarlet*. But when Holmes and Watson are talking about that story in the first chapter of *The Sign of Four*, and Holmes is criticizing it, Dr Watson writes: 'More than once during the years that I lived with him in Baker

Street I had observed that a small vanity underlay my companion's quiet and didactic manner. I made no remark, however, but sat nursing my wounded leg. I had had a Jezail bullet through it some time before, and though it did not prevent me from walking, it ached wearily at every change of the weather.' Dr Watson, and his creator, Dr Arthur Conan Doyle, both medical men, really should not have confused their anatomy to the extent of making a wound in the shoulder a wound in the leg!

* * *

The most priceless howler in fiction must be that in one of Ouida's innumerable novels, which were immensely popular about the seventies and eighties of the last century. She was Mlle Louise de la Ramée, but always wrote under the pseudonym of Ouida, which was a childish mispronunciation of Louise. I never read any of her books, and I suppose no one reads them nowadays, but somewhere or other I have seen it said that in the description of a boat-race in one of her novels she made the remarkable statement that 'they all rowed fast, but Stroke rowed the fastest of them all'!

SOME QUEER LITANIES

THERE are many traditional sayings which take the form of a litany. Some of these—most of them, in fact—are popular phrases with a humorous cast. But some are more seriously meant. The most moving of all these is the petition that was inserted in the liturgy by the monks who lived in the monasteries near the northern coasts of France, in the earlier Middle Ages; '*A furore Normannorum, libera nos, Domine!*' 'From the fury of the Northmen, deliver us, O Lord!' Many a time the northern marauders would land from their 'long ships' and strike inland, burning, robbing, ravaging, murdering wherever they went, with a special hatred in their heathen hearts for the monasteries and the churches. There are several villages on the coast of Lincolnshire where the stones at the base of the church tower still show plain traces of fire. The Norsemen tried to burn them down, very likely with the inhabitants of the village who had taken refuge there inside, because the church was the only stone building, and the tower the only structure capable of serving either as a place of refuge or as a place of defence.

This, by the way, was not unknown in much later days. The Border between England and Scotland was a debatable land for many centuries, and raids from both the north and the south were fairly frequent. There is an interesting survival in the Parish Church of Bedale. The only entrance into the tower is from inside the church. There is now a wooden door, but behind it you can see the grooves in the stonework where an iron portcullis was let down when the folk of the village had taken refuge in the tower because of a Scottish raid. The wooden door could be burned away: the portcullis of iron could not.

*　　*　　*

Another medieval example is the relic of what was quite an important episode in the thirteenth century. It is a long and complex story. In the University of Paris—then the most famous seat of learning in Europe—there was a great dispute which grew out of the jealousy between the Seculars (the ordinary clergy) and the Mendicants (the Franciscans and Dominicans). The Seculars complained that they were being impoverished because of the way that crowds of people resorted to the churches of the Friars. This animosity got into the universities, where there was the same resentment against the popularity of Franciscan and Dominican teachers. Several things brought this to a head. There was a riot in which the students of the University were involved, and several of them were arrested. The University demanded redress, and ceased all lectures to enforce the protest. But the Dominican doctors went on with their lectures. When the University opened its doors again there was an attempt to impose an oath of obedience upon the Mendicants, which they refused to take. There was then an appeal to Rome, which took the part of the Friars. Then William of St Amour was sent to Rome to represent the other side to Pope Innocent IV. A sudden change of front followed and in November 1254 the Pope issued a Bull which was a complete victory for the University and the Secular clergy, and a severe defeat for the Friars. Every Dominican was then ordered to pray daily for the annulment of this 'most cruel edict'. The next events were dramatic. Innocent IV died on the 7th of December, about a fortnight after the issue of the Bull. It was widely believed that his death was the work of the Dominicans. A new Pope, Alexander IV, was speedily elected. Within ten days after his accession he had revoked the Bull of his predecessor, and a few months later another Bull decided the whole dispute in favour of the Dominicans. Then it passed into a byword at the Curia in Rome: '*A litaniis Praedicatorum, libera nos, Domine!*' 'From the prayers of the Preachers [i.e. the Dominicans], Lord, deliver us!'

There is another suffrage also that is associated with the Friars, for when some of the early followers of St Francis who were sent out into Germany and Hungary in 1217 returned the next year to Italy and reported their failure and their sufferings, it is said the Friars added to their litany the prayer: 'From the heresy of the Lombards, and from the ferocity of the Germans, Lord, deliver us!'

* * *

Other sayings of this kind reflect upon the character of particular races and families. It is said that there used to be an inscription over the West Gate of the city of Galway in Ireland: 'From the fury of the O'Flaherties, good Lord, deliver us!' Gibbon, in *The Decline and Fall of the Roman Empire*, has some remarks on the traditional cunning of the Athenians, and adds that it is a proverbial saying in the East: 'From the Jews of Thessalonica, the Turks of Negropont, and the Greeks of Athens, good Lord, deliver us!' In the parish register of the village church at Darton in Yorkshire there is a curious entry. The Vicar of the parish during the Civil War was John Heathfield. He was evidently no Puritan, and he has left a notice of himself in the register, with the addition of a prayer (in dubious Latin): '*A dolis rotundi capitis, libera me, Domine, et Judae suavium det Deus ut caveam.* 'From the deceits of the Roundheads, Lord deliver me, and God grant that I may beware of the kiss of Judas.'

There is a byword about a famous Scottish family—'the muckle-mou'ed Murrays'. It is said that for many generations this feature of the family did persist. It will be remembered that this comes into the ancestral story of Sir Walter Scott. Sir Gideon Murray, who lived in the time of King James VI, had a daughter Agnes who was supposed to possess this family heritage of a very large mouth. William Scott of Haden was caught in a foray on the Murray lands, and given the choice of marrying the 'muckle-mouthed' damsel or being hanged. Like a wise man, he chose the former alternative. James Hogg, the Ettrick

Shepherd, has a ballad on the theme, and Browning also has a poem on it, but he gives a pleasant twist to the story, and calls the maiden 'muckle-mouthed Meg'. But there was another byword about the family—'the wind of the Murrays'. Here 'wind' is used in the old Scottish sense of boasting and bravado. Now, there was a small estate in Perthshire by the name of Cultoquey, which had belonged to the Maxton family for five hundred years. This in itself was something of a miracle, for the estate was surrounded by the lands of powerful neighbours, none too scrupulous in that territory and in the days of old, and perhaps none too obliging in more modern times. It is said that the Maxton who owned Cultoquey in the early nineteenth century used to repeat every morning at the end of his devotions some lines in which the neighbouring landlords were characterized, not too sympathetically:

From the greed of the Campbells,
From the ire of the Drummonds,
From the pride of the Grahams,
From the wind of the Murrays,
Good Lord, deliver us!

These families are said to have taken this in good part, when it became known, except the Murrays, and the Duke of Atholl invited Maxton to dinner and dared him to repeat the lines. Maxton did so, quite unperturbed, and the Duke, half amused and half angry, said : 'Take care, Cultie, for the future to omit my name in your morning devotions, else I shall certainly crop your ears for your boldness.' Maxton coolly drank his glass of wine, and said: 'That's *wind*, my lord Duke!'

* * *

Probably the most familiar of all these sayings is that which was a kind of thieves' litany years ago: 'From Hell and Hull and Halifax, good Lord, deliver me!' It is said that there is historic ground for the aversion of criminals to these two towns. Halifax had very severe laws in the Middle Ages against the theft of cloth. Anyone who stole cloth to the value of elevenpence was beheaded, and a kind of primitive guillotine, invented by 'a fat Friar', was used for the purpose. Hull had also some drastic laws against vagrants, who were whipped out of the town. I quoted the byword in an article some years ago, and the late Dr Albert Peel sent me a variant version of it, which made the localities, 'Hull, *Elland*, Halifax'. Elland is a town near Halifax, of course.

One of these sayings concerns trade conditions in the seventeenth century. The Statute of Apprentices of 1563 required that every man professing 'a trade or mystery' must serve a seven-years' apprenticeship. This regulation apparently was not well enforced, and in 1619 James I began the practice of selling exemptions to those who had not been apprenticed to the trade they were carrying on. There was strong feeling about this, particularly among the weavers of Essex, and there were renewed protests in 1654 when the Commonwealth gave all who had served in the army the right to engage in any handicraft or trade. The wool-combers had a song, one stanza of which ran:

From such as would our rights invade
Or would intrude into our trade,
And break the law Queen Betty made,
Libera nos, Domine.

* * *

It would be a pity to omit two traditional suffrages that have a weird quality which seems to belong to a dark winter's night. One is from Cornwall: 'From witches and wizards, and long-tailed buzzards, and creeping things that run along hedge-bottoms, good Lord, deliver us!' The other is from Yorkshire, and it is equally eerie, 'From ghoulies and ghaisties, and lang-leggit beasties, and things that go *bump* in the night, good Lord, deliver us!'

* * *

One of the most amusing sayings of this type comes from D. L. Moody, the famous American evangelist whose missions brought so much good to this land seventy or eighty years ago. He used to say: 'From long-haired men and short-haired women, good Lord, deliver us!' The saying has lost half its point through a change in feminine fashions. There is nothing odd about ladies who wear their hair short today: the fashion has become so general that there is nothing noticeable in it. There is still something Bohemian, and out of the ordinary, about a man with long hair, and a couple of generations ago there was something ultra-modern and defiant about a woman with short hair. Moody was blessed with a very sane outlook, and, like all manly men, he feared and shunned the type of persons who think of themselves as 'advanced' and are thought of by others as affected!

PEPYS AND WESLEY

NO two books could be much more unlike than Pepys's *Diary* and Wesley's *Journal*, but there is one link and one likeness between them. The link is that interesting eighteenth-century personality, John Byrom. The likeness lies in the fact that both books were originally written in shorthand, and partly in cipher, and the decipherment of the whole *Diary* of Pepys and of the early *Diaries* of Wesley are feats that have no parallel, as far as I know, in the history of English literature.

Pepys's famous *Diary* extends from the beginning of 1659-60 to the middle of 1669. He left his library—it included the six volumes of his *Diary*—to his nephew, John Jackson, but it was all to go eventually to Magdalene College at Cambridge, where Pepys had been a student (and where the only contemporary record of him, by the way, is that on the 12th of October 1653 he was admonished for having been 'scandalously overserved with drink the night before'). On the death of Jackson in 1724 the bequest to Magdalene took effect, and Pepys's Library was housed in a large room in the College buildings, where it remained until 1849. Then for five years it was in the Master's Lodge, and since 1854 it has been in a fireproof room in the Pepysian Buildings. Until recent days very few people seem to have visited the Library, and only once, I think, is there any reference to the *Diary*. Ralph Leycester (often called Peter, or Sir Peter, in what was intended, I suppose, as a humorous allusion to his grandfather, Sir Peter Leycester, Bart.) was interested in shorthand, and was the leading disciple of Dr Byrom. In 1728 he went to the Library at Magdalene to examine Pepys's collection of books on shorthand. He wrote to Byrom and told him of the visit, and mentioned, quite incidentally, that he had seen the *Diary* there. Now this is specially interesting.

* * *

John Byrom was an extraordinary person. He wrote a great deal of verse, some of it quaint and witty, and he wrote the famous Christmas hymn, 'Christians awake, salute the happy morn'. He was also a staunch Jacobite and wrote the famous epigram:

God bless the King, God bless the faith's defender;
God bless—no harm in blessing—the Pretender;
But who Pretender is, and who is King—
God bless us all—is quite another thing!

When the Pretender got as far as Manchester on his march south, however, Byrom was prudent enough not to commit himself. There is another epigram of Byrom's that is well known. It is upon the famous musical rivalries in the London of the eighteenth century:

Some say, compared to Buononcini,
That Mynheer Handel's but a ninny;
Others aver that he to Handel
Is scarcely fit to hold a candle:
Strange all this difference should be
'Twixt tweedle-dum and tweedle-dee!

As all this is enough to show, Byrom was very versatile, and there were still some more sides to him. He was deeply interested in the mystics, especially Antoinette Bourignon, Jakob Boehme, and William Law, whom he visited at King's Cliffe.

Now, it was Byrom's shorthand that the Wesleys used. John Wesley learned it, on his brother Charles's advice, when they were in Georgia. It is said that Byrom invented his system while he was in Cambridge, and later on, when he had to give up his Fellowship at Trinity on his marriage, he turned to shorthand to make a living. In 1742 he obtained from Parliament the sole privilege of teaching his system for twenty-one years. His shorthand is said to be clear, and characterized by simple strokes and an absence of arbitrary characters, but it cannot be written rapidly, and on that account has passed out of modern use.

* * *

Now, when Leycester came across the manuscript of Pepys's *Diary* in the Library at Cambridge, he wrote to Byrom, who was regarded as the greatest stenographer in England, as follows: 'I spent the last week at Cambridge. Whilst I was there I went to see a curious collection of books bequeathed to Magdalene College by the late Mr Pepys. In the catalogue I met with a book entitled *Shorthand Collection*, and would gladly have seen it, but the gentleman who showed us the library being a stranger, and unacquainted with the method of the catalogue, could not find it. Mr Hadderton tells [*sic*] it is a collection of shorthand books containing above a hundred and fifty different methods. In searching for this book we found five large volumes, quarto, being a journal of Mr Pepys; I did not know the method, but they were writ very plain, and the proper names in common character. If you think it worth while to make Cambridge on your way to London you will meet with these and I doubt not several other shorthand curiosities in the Magdalene Library. I had not time, and was loth to be troublesome to the library keeper, otherwise I would have deciphered some of the journal.' Byrom did not rise to the opportunity, or he might have been the one to give Pepys's *Diary* to the world.

* * *

When Evelyn's *Diary* was published in the year 1818 the mention of Pepys in it attracted the attention of the Master of Magdalene, whereupon he showed the volumes of the *Diary* to his relative, Lord Grenville. Now, Lord Grenville knew something of shorthand and ciphers, and he deciphered a few pages, and gave them into the hands of John Smith, an undergraduate of St John's, who was charged with the task of deciphering the whole *Diary*. Smith eventually became the Rector of Baldock, in Hertfordshire, and nearly forty years after he had completed his task of decipherment—it took him three years—he wrote dolefully of 'how difficult, how laborious, and how unprofitable' it was. He would have felt still more mournful about it if he had realized that, reposing in the Library at Magdalene there was a copy of Shelton's *Tachygraphy*, a book published in 1641 which contained the system of shorthand used by Pepys, and also a shorthand account, taken down from the lips of Charles II, of his escape after the Battle of Worcester, with a longhand transcript, and that these would have given a complete clue to the *Diary*. The *Diary* first appeared, under the editorship of Lord Draybrooke, in 1825.

* * *

The greatest exploit of this kind during the present century, and the only one at all comparable to Smith's decipherment of Pepys, is a feat that has a special interest for Methodists. John Wesley's *Journal* was compiled from the diaries which he kept from 1725 to 1791. Many of these are lost, and, it is to be feared, hopelessly lost, but the series is reasonably complete from 1725 to 1734, from 1735 to 1737, and from 1739 to 1741. Now, these manuscript diaries are written in a cipher, and, in the later volumes, in a system of eighteenth-century shorthand, mixed with the cipher. We know that Wesley taught Weston's shorthand at Oxford, though he did not use it himself. He used Byrom's shorthand. Part of the Georgia diary and all the latter diaries are in that system.

Now, the task of deciphering Wesley's early diaries was a very formidable one, and might have been thought impossible. But it was accomplished by the Rev. Nehemiah Curnock, the Editor of the Standard Edition of Wesley's *Journal*, whose name deserves most honourable remembrance on that score alone, but also for many other reasons. Mr Curnock learned Byrom's system of shorthand—no small task in itself—and by a combination of intense study and inspired guesses managed to interpret the cipher. It is interesting to learn that one of the clues to the cipher came to Mr Curnock in a dream!

He has left a fascinating account of the whole business of decipherment in the Standard Edition of the *Journal*. It was the complicated cipher that Wesley had devised for his own use that presented the major difficulty. It would have been a fairly straightforward enterprise to read off the shorthand, though it was an obsolete system, when once you had learned it, but the shorthand was mixed with arbitrary signs, and Greek letters, and abbreviations, and, worst of all, a shifting set of equivalences, so that a letter might stand for any one of six others in some cases. Mr Curnock's work in solving all these complexities was a really extraordinary exploit, and I have always felt that it deserved a great deal more notice, and a great deal more praise, than it ever received. Why did not one of the universities acknowledge it with an honorary degree?

CHILDREN'S SAYINGS

IF you are happy enough to have little children around you let me give you some good advice. Keep a record of their remarkable sayings when they are very young. For all small children say remarkable things from time to time, and if you write these down at the moment you will not lose them. It will be interesting to recall these childish utterances later on, and sometimes they are strikingly suggestive, in a psychological sense. There are extant some very interesting collections of such children's sayings, notably those by Lady Glenconner and by Mr William Canton, and some striking examples are also to be found in Professor Sully's book, *Studies of Childhood*.

* * *

I have long been convinced that the intelligence of small children is grossly underestimated by most adults. We are often told, for example, that young children cannot grasp some of the greater truths of religion; when in church they are not supposed, therefore, to be able to understand the sermon, and so in many places are turned out into the street in the middle of the morning service. I am quite sure that all this is wrong. I can remember, as a very small boy, pondering over what I now know are some of the greatest mysteries in life and in religion. Most children do this, but naturally they have not always the language to tell the grown-ups what they are puzzling about, and I think they are also checked by an instinctive shyness in these matters.

* * *

Some of the recorded sayings of children are enough to prove what I have said as to the depth of their secret speculations about what are really profound philosophical and religious issues. A little girl once said to Mr Allanson Picton: 'Please tell me why there was ever anything at all?' That raises every ultimate question that the human intellect can face, in a single drastic query. Another child said, at 'the animated hour of the bath', 'You know, everything belongs to something else, if you think about it,' and then proceeded to chant cheerfully:

O, the towel and the bath,
And the bath and the soap,
And the soap was the fat,
And the fat was the pig,
And the pig was the bran,
And the bran makes sausages,
And Man eats the sausages,
And God gets man.

Here is a quaint and childish expression of the truth that all things in the Universe are interrelated and interdependent, and, moreover, that there is a hierarchy of being reaching up through all living things, from the vegetable to the animal, the animal to the human, and the human to the Divine.

* * *

A small boy remarked: 'If I'd gone upstairs, could God make it that I hadn't?' That reminds me of a poignant passage in one of Heywood's plays, which has remained in my memory for more than forty years. When Frankford (in *A Woman Killed with Kindness*) sees what he knows is the wreck of all that he holds dear, he exclaims:

O God, O God, that it were possible
To undo things done; to call back yesterday;
That time could turn up his swift sandy glass,
To untell the days, and to redeem these hours!

That passage is worthy of Shakespeare in its pathos and in its profundity. Yet that very paradox was in the mind of the child who wanted to know whether God could undo a thing that had been done. Another little boy, aged three, repeatedly asked, 'Where has yesterday gone?' and 'Why does counting never end?' Now, these last questions, of course, involve the problem of time and the concept of infinity, as the former query involves the whole relation of time and reality.

* * *

Many a child's word about religion is profoundly suggestive. Thus Professor Sully relates that a little boy remarked to his mother that if he could say what he liked to God, it would be: 'Love me when I am naughty.' Surely that is *testimonium animae naturaliter Christianae*, in the great phrase of Tertullian, 'the witness of a soul naturally Christian,' for what does the Gospel mean but that *while we were yet sinners* Christ died for us? Another child said: 'When I say my prayers I always *see* everything. When I say, "Deliver us from evil", I see God going out with a spear to fight Satan; and when I say, "Forgive us our trespasses", I see Him with a big rubber cleaning a blackboard.' Another little boy of seven repeated the text, *The blood of Jesus Christ His Son cleanseth us from all sin.* Then he thought for a while, and said: 'I see how it is: the blood of Jesus is God's india-rubber; when it is rubbed over the page of the book where our sins are written, it takes them all away.' This sounds crude and childish, but it is not so far removed from the Apostle's words: 'having forgiven you all trespasses, blotting out the handwriting of ordinances that was against us.'

The problem of evil often exercises the mind of the child. A little boy of five years old said he wished he could be God for five minutes. When he was asked why, and what he would do, he said: 'I would kill the Devil.' A little girl of three made a more evangelical approach to the difficulty. 'Mother,' she said solemnly, 'has the Devil got a Saviour?'

* * *

A five-year-old boy, whose father was evidently a soldier, was distressed by the story of the Crucifixion. 'Oh, Mother,' he said, 'if Father had been there *he* would have sworded off their heads!' Precisely the same kind of naïve reaction is told of more than one warrior of olden days. It is related of Crillon, called by Henri IV 'the bravest of the brave' that the gallant old soldier was in church, listening to the story of the Passion, and growing more and more enraged as he heard of all that was inflicted upon our Lord, he drew his sword and cried out: 'Where wert *thou*, Crillon?' (*Où étais-tu, Crillon?*) There is a somewhat similar story about Clovis. When the king, formerly a pagan, resolved to declare himself a Christian, his wife Clotilda sent for Remigius, the Bishop of Rheims, who began to instruct Clovis in the facts of the gospel. When he spoke of the Crucifixion Clovis angrily exclaimed: 'Had I only been there with my Franks, I would have taught those Jews a lesson!'

* * *

It is interesting to note the child's attitude toward words, which is very like that of savages today, and of primitive man in the far past. They cannot readily separate the name and the thing, and always regard a word as a sort of entity in its own right. One of Lady Glenconner's children remarked thoughtfully one night: 'I think it is the name that is so frightening. I don't like to say it: it is so terrible, *Death*' (he shuddered as he lay in bed). 'I wish it wasn't *called* that! I don't think I should mind it so much if it were called Hig.' The child did not (and, of course, could not) realize that Hig, or any other vocable, if it had become the name of what we call Death, would have acquired all the associations of mortality, and so would have been equally terrible to him. The townsman in *Punch* who was watching the swine rooting in the dirt, and remarked disgustedly. 'Ah, no wonder they're called *pigs*!' was in precisely the same mental attitude as the child: the one could not dissociate terror, and the other could not dissociate filth, from the word 'death' and the word 'pig', though any other combination of letters would have acquired those associations just the same, if it had come to be the name of the thing.

And yet one wonders if that is the whole truth. For it is recorded that a little girl, who was having Kingsley's *Heroes* read to her, asked her mother, whenever the Gorgons were mentioned, to say instead 'the Ladies'. She said she did not like the *sound* of the word Gorgon: 'It made her draw herself together.' One remembers Milton:

> *Orcus and Ades and the dreaded name*
> *Of Demogorgon.*

On the other hand, a small child, after he had been put to bed, and the light was extinguished, said: 'Isn't *Christ* a beautiful word? It shines like a bright stone.'

* * *

One thing that constantly appears in the sayings of children is the curious notion that adults as they grow older will grow smaller, and revert to childhood, so to speak. A boy of three and a half years old said to his mother: 'When I am big then you will be little, then I will carry you about and dress you and put you to sleep.' A little girl, who was not so amiable at the moment, said: 'When I am a big girl and you are a little girl I shall whip you just as you whipped me now!' Professor Sully says that he has not been able to find any such notion in primitive folk-lore. I can think of one or two faint parallels, or what seem so. There used to be a belief in Cornwall, for example, that the fairies were the ancient Druids, who refused to accept the Christian faith, and as a punishment grew smaller and smaller as they grew older and older, with the passing years.

* * *

Naturally enough, children often misunderstand words that they hear, sometimes with quaint results. One little boy looked sad when other children spoke of their birthdays, and said sorrowfully: 'Oh, John's birthday fell down; John's birthday tummle over!' No one could fathom this trouble until, one day he murmured: 'John's birthday knocked over!' Then the grown-ups saw what he meant, and were able to console him. He had been told that his birthday was *in October* (*knocked over!*). A six-year-old girl learned in her geography lesson that Yarmouth was celebrated for 'the curing of herrings'. 'Oh, how funny it must be,' she said, 'to see the little ill herrings sitting round *getting better*.'

JANUARY

THE month of January derives its name from Janus, the Roman deity who presided over doors and entrances, whence also comes the word 'Janitor' for a door-keeper—a word much more in use in America than it is here. Janus was represented with two faces, or sometimes with four faces. The two faces are supposed to betoken that the god knew both the past and the future; the four faces that he ruled over the four seasons of the year. He is called *Martialis*, because he had to do with war, and his temples were always open when Rome was engaged in hostilities, and closed in time of peace. He had a special relation to the year, and is sometimes shown with the number 300 in one hand, and the number 65 in the other. His principal festival was on New Year's Day.

* * *

January is perhaps as rich in popular rites and traditional observances as any month in the year except December, and some of these are the aftermath of Christmas. But there is one rather curious usage which is manifestly pre-Christian and prehistoric. It flourishes even today in the north of England: it is the superstitious rite of the 'first-foot'. The first person who crosses the threshold of your house as soon as the old year is past is a kind of omen. He will bring you good luck or bad luck throughout the year that is beginning. In some places he is supposed to bring a small gift, a coin, or a bit of bread, or a bit of cheese, or a piece of coal. The point here is obviously that the year should begin by things which represent food and warmth and wealth coming into the house, so that good things will come in all through the year. The other side of this is that there would be great reluctance to let anything go out of the house as the first event of the year. (This particular kind of superstition was found, by the way, in ancient Rome.) But the most intriguing point about the 'first-foot' was that it must be a dark-complexioned man; not a woman, and not a fair person, if he was to bring luck. This is very significant. The earliest inhabitants of this land of whom we know anything were a small, dark people, generally called Iberian, who were still in the Stone Age. It is probable that this race still survives in some parts of Ireland, Wales, and western Scotland as shorter and swarthier individuals. The Iberians were succeeded by the Celts, who were tall and fair. Now when an aboriginal folk have been conquered by a more advanced race, they are always regarded by their conquerors as possessed of magical powers, and therefore able to bring good fortune. That is why the 'first-foot' must be of dark complexion. I knew people—intelligent and religious people too—fifty years ago in the county of Durham who would have been rather upset if a fair-complexioned man (or, still worse, a woman) had been the first caller after midnight on the 31st of December.

* * *

There are several interesting festivals, sacred and secular, that fall in the month of January. The first notable date after New Year's Day was the Feast of the Epiphany on the 6th of January. This was popularly known as Twelfth Day or Twelfth Night; that is to say, it was twelve days after Christmas, and it marked the end of the revelries of Christmastide. It will be remembered that the festival gave the name to one of Shakespeare's comedies, probably because the play was first performed on that date. Pepys saw it on Twelfth Night, 1662-3, and complained that it was 'not related at all to the name or day'.

The day after, the 7th of January, was quaintly called St Distaff's Day, because it was supposed to be the time when women resumed their spinning after the Christmas holidays.

They seem to have taken up the task rather half-heartedly, for a popular rhyme says:

On St Distaff's Day
Neither work nor play,

and Herrick has a poem on St Distaff's Day in which he also implies that work did not really start in earnest until the day after.

The masculine parallel to St Distaff's Day was Plough Monday, the first Monday after Twelfth Day, which was a sort of final holiday after which the ploughman resumed his work on the land. A plough was dressed up with ribbons, and a number of men were yoked to it: they were called 'plough bullocks', as bullocks were used in the olden days to draw the plough. They went round the village, and collected contributions in money, as well as food and drink, at the farmhouses. If any farmer were so miserly (and so unwise) as to refuse a gift, the ground in front of his residence was ploughed up. In addition to the men who dragged the plough there were a number of mummers. One was called 'the Bessy', and he carried the collecting box; one was 'the Fool'; and others danced a Morris-dance, or blew loud blasts on bullocks' horns. I believe that the Plough Monday celebration still survives in some parts of the country.

* * *

The Feast of St Hilary falls on the 14th of January. It has given a name to Hilary Term, in the Law Courts and in the University of Oxford. St Hilary was Bishop of Poitiers from about the year 350 to his death in 368. He was a really great man. Originally a pagan, he became a Christian, it would appear, largely by way of the study of philosophy. Later he was the leading theologian of the West on the side of orthodoxy in the Arian dispute; indeed, he was the counterpart of Athanasius in the East. He was banished because of his defence of the Nicene doctrine, and spent five years in the Asiatic provinces—an exile which he characteristically used to improve his knowledge of Greek. It was in this period that he wrote his treatise, *On the Trinity*. That work contains one of the most suggestive sentences, in my judgement, that was ever written about the doctrine: '*Aeternitas in Patre, Species in Imagine, Usus in Munere*' ('Eternity in the Father, Form in the Image, Use in the Gift'). Nearly all that is vital in the doctrine of the Trinity is contained in that pregnant sentence of nine Latin words.

* * *

The most curious ecclesiastical festival in the month is that of St Almachius, in the martyrology for the 1st of January. He is a saint who never existed. Some copyist of long ago, finding in the Breviary an abbreviation of *Sanctum Almanacum* (the sacred calendar) in the form of St Alm'ac', or something like that, prefixed to the list of festivals, thought it referred to a saint, and duly entered him on the first day of the year as St Almachius. Then a legend came into existence which related that St Almachius suffered martyrdom at Rome during the prefecture of Alpius, at the beginning of the fifth century. He is said to have protested (like St Telemachus) against the gladiatorial shows, and to have been slain by the incensed gladiators. But all that is baseless: the plain fact is that *the Almanack* has been mistakenly enrolled among the saints of Rome!

* * *

An Act of Parliament in the reign of George the Second reformed the calendar and provided that henceforth the legal year should begin on the 1st of January, and not on the 25th of March as heretofore, and that the day following the 2nd of September 1752 should be reckoned the 14th, thus omitting eleven days. This has a definite bearing on the persistent tradition of a snowy Christmas, which still pervades our Christmas cards, our Christmas decorations, and our Christmas carols.

Between 1841 and 1924 there were only eighteen years, or rather less than one in five, when snow fell on Christmas Eve, Christmas Day, or Boxing Day. But up to 1752 Christmas Day fell on what is now the 6th of January, and I have often noted that when there has been no snow at Christmas, we have often had it soon afterward, within the first few days of the New Year. Thus in 1942, for example, we had a mild Christmas here in the Midlands, but the ground was white with snow on the 30th of December, and on the 2nd of January 1943, and again on the 5th and 6th, which would have meant a white Christmas under the old calendar.

The omission of the eleven days brought England into line with the reformed calendar which had been introduced by Pope Gregory XIII in the sixteenth century. That reform had been well received in Catholic countries, where the Papal authority was respected, and the more ignorant of the populace were reassured (if they needed to be) by the fact that miracles supposed to happen on particular dates were obliging enough to accept the new reckoning. Thus the liquefaction of the blood of St Januarius at Naples, which always happened on the 19th of September, happened according to the new style, after the change was made. The English population were not as well disposed to the reformed calendar, probably because it was a Papal reform. Many ignorant folk seem to have thought that they were really being defrauded of eleven days, and it is said that unpopular politicians were frequently greeted with the cry: 'Who stole the eleven days? Give us back the eleven days!'

* * *

Now, the famous legend of Glastonbury—

where the winter thorn
Blossoms at Christmas, mindful of our Lord—

relates that Joseph of Arimathea came to the place, and thrust his staff into the ground at Wyrral-hill (popularly Weary-all-hill).

The staff struck root and grew into a tree which budded and blossomed every Christmas. When the calendar was changed a great crowd of people gathered at midnight on Christmas Eve to see whether the thorn blossomed. It did not, and another crowd mustered on the 5th of January (which was Christmas Eve according to the unreformed calendar, 'when it blowed as usual'. This is recorded in the *Gentlemen's Magazine* for January 1753. The people, of course, regarded this as proof positive that the old calendar was right! There is still a tree in the grounds of Glastonbury Abbey that is supposed to be a descendant of the Holy Thorn.

THE EPIPHANY

THE first great festival of the Church after the beginning of the year is the Feast of the Epiphany, or, as the *Book of Common Prayer* further describes it, the Manifestation of Christ to the Gentiles. The Epiphany—the Greek word *epiphaneia* means 'manifestation'—was always a prominent festival in the east. There, in fact, it was almost the equivalent of what Christmas was in the West, for in the early centuries the feast of Christmas was peculiar to the Latin Church. Chrysostom tells us that it was not introduced at Antioch until about the year 375. On the other hand, the festival of the Epiphany appears for the first time in the west about the year 350, when there is a mention of it in Gaul. In the east Clement of Alexandria refers to it a hundred and fifty years earlier. In the Oriental churches the Epiphany was regarded as being a threefold commemoration of the Nativity, the Adoration of the Magi, and the Baptism of Christ. Sometimes the first miracle at Cana of Galilee is also included in the remembrance. The idea seems to be that each of these was, in its own way, a 'manifestation' of the glory and power of Christ. It is interesting to note that there are allusions to the Adoration of the Wise Men, to the Baptism of our Lord, and to the miracle of the water made into wine, in the hymn *Crudelis Herodes* appointed for Epiphany in the *Breviary*, as well as in other parts of the liturgy for the festival. But in the Western Church the feast became more and more restricted to a commemoration of the Wise Men. Thus the six sermons on the Epiphany of St Augustine, and the eight sermons on the same subject of St Leo the Great, are all mainly concerned with the Magi. (The fourth lesson in the Office for the Epiphany in the *Breviary*, by the way, is from the second of these sermons of St Leo.) No doubt the translation of the supposed relics of the

Magi to Milan about 316 gave a great impetus to the tendency which made the Epiphany mainly the feast of the Wise Men.

*   *   *

There has been an enormous accretion of legend around the story of the Magi. They were generally supposed to be three in number, which is an obvious inference from the three gifts, though some oriental forms of the legend make them twelve. The traditional names of the Magi occur first of all, apparently, in Bede, in the form Melchior, Gaspar (or Caspar), and Balthasar. The belief that they were kings appears clearly first of all in Caesarius of Arles. It became the universal belief in the Middle Ages, and *Festum Trium Regum*, the Feast of the Three Kings, was a common synonym in the West for the Feast of the Epiphany. The Dutch still call it *Drie koningendag*, Three-Kings-Day, and the Danes *Hellig-tre-kongersdag*, Holy-Three-Kings-Day. This notion no doubt derived from two passages in the Old Testament. One is Isaiah 60^{3}: 'And nations shall come to thy light, and kings to the brightness of thy rising.' The other is Psalm 62^{10-11}: 'The kings of Tarshish and of the isles shall bring presents: the kings of Sheba and Seba shall offer gifts.' So the legend says that one of the Magi came from Tharsis, one from Saba, and one from Arabia. Each had been warned of the approaching birth of Christ by a miraculous portent. Gaspar had an ostrich that laid two eggs, from which were hatched a lion and a lamb. Balthasar had a garden in which a flower blossomed suddenly, and from the flower a bird flew away. Melchior had a child born to him, and the babe spoke at birth and prophesied his own death and the birth of Christ within thirty-three days. The Three Kings met on the way to Bethlehem, having known nothing of each other before. One was twenty years old, one forty, and one sixty, so that they represented each period of human life; youth, maturity, and age. They came, according to one form of the legend, from Europe, Asia, and Africa, and so represented the three continents known to the ancient world, and the three races of mankind, white, yellow, and black. Their gifts were gold, as given in tribute to a king; frankincense, as given in worship to God; and myrrh, as prophetic of our Lord's death.

The legend adds that the Three Kings became followers of Christ, and died in India while partaking of the Lord's Supper. Their bodies were found, after a search instituted by St Helena, and were conveyed to Constantinople, and buried in the Church of St Sophia. Later, the story goes, these relics were presented to Eustorgius, the Bishop of Milan, who was a Greek by birth. This was in the fourth century. Then when the Emperor Barbarossa sacked Milan in 1163, the Archbishop Reinald carried off the remains of the Three Kings to Cologne, where the relics are still preserved in a golden reliquary in the Cathedral, and where they are still venerated. The legend has inspired the little poem of Heine, '*Die heil'gen drei Kön'ge aus Morgenland*', one of the most beautiful things he ever wrote. The invocation, 'O ye Three Holy Kings, Gaspar, Melchior, Balthasar, Pray for us now and in the hour of death!' (especially if the words were written down, and the writing had touched the relics of the Three Kings of Cologne) was long regarded as an almost infallible charm. The Three Kings were specially the patron saints of travellers, naturally enough, in view of their long pilgrimage to Bethlehem. I have read somewhere that formerly it was usual to carve over the door of an inn in Franconia and Carinthia the letters C.M.B., which signify the traditional names of the Three Kings, Gaspar, Melchior, and Balthasar.

* * *

Such are some of the quaint and interesting details in the legendary lore that has gathered around the story of the Wise Men. What are the probable facts? The incident, one of the most beautiful details in the record of the Nativity, is related only in St Matthew's Gospel, and the word used there to describe the Wise Men is *magoi*, *magi*, closely related to our 'magic'. The word is also used in the Acts of the Apostles of Bar-Jesus and Elymas, the sorcerors, and (in the verbal form) of Simon, who 'used sorcery' and 'bewitched the people with sorceries'. The word is possibly of Babylonian origin, and seems to be applied to priests, physicians, astrologers, soothsayers, sorcerers—all who were supposed to possess esoteric knowledge.

Where did the Magi come from? Far and away the most probable conjecture, it seems to me, is that they came from Persia. That is expressly stated by Clement of Alexandria and Chrysostom, among the Fathers. According to Herodotus the Magi were a Median tribe that had attempted to usurp authority in Persia, and had failed, but retained a good deal of importance because they were the priestly caste, rather like the Levites in Israel. Thus they were closely identified with Zoroastrian religion. It is said that there used to be on the western façade of the Church of the Nativity at Bethlehem a mosaic, dating from the days of Justinian, which showed the Adoration of the Magi, and that the Persians under Chosroes, recognizing their own national costumes in the dress of the Magi, forbore to destroy the church.

What of the star? It was suggested by Kepler, the great astronomer, that the heavenly sign was a conjunction of Jupiter and Saturn in the year 7 B.C., similar to the one which he witnessed in 1604, when an evanescent star of peculiar colour also appeared, as he thought it might have done sixteen centuries before. Later astronomers have showed that the conjunction of the two planets happened thrice in the year 7 B.C.—a phenomenon which must have been as impressive as it is rare. The most probable date of the Nativity is thought to be between 7 B.C. and 5 B.C., and the appearance of the astronomical portent in the former year is a striking fact, to say the least. The curious detail has been pointed out that Abrabanel, the Jewish commentator of the fifteenth century, states that in the belief of Jewish astrologers a conjunction of these two planets was to be the sign of the Messiah's advent. It was believed from very early times that the star had been foretold in the Scriptures. Both Origen and Irenaeus suggest that the Magi saw in the star the fulfilment of Balaam's prophecy in Numbers 24[17]: 'I see him, but not now; I behold him, but not nigh: there shall come forth a star out of Jacob, and a sceptre shall rise out of Israel.' One detail of the later legend affirms that the Wise Men were descendants of Balaam, and that the memory of his prophecy had been preserved by their forbears.

* * *

How much poorer the world would have been in many ways if the visit of the Magi to Bethlehem had never happened, or if it had never been recorded! Many a great picture of the Adoration would be blank canvas, and many a great passage in the world's poetry would be blank paper. We ought to be thankful from the depth of our hearts not only for the amazing fact of the Incarnation, but for all the lovely incidents that gather around the birth of our Lord, and not least that the Wise Men from the east came with their gifts:

See how from far upon the eastern road
The star-led wizards haste with odours sweet!

IF CHRIST IS NOT RISEN

An Easter Meditation

OUR faith in the Resurrection of our Lord is not only vital to our creed: it is vital to everything that is best in the experience of humanity. It is essential to religion, for all our religion centres in Christ; in what He said and what He did and what He was. His teaching is our guide; His life is our pattern; His death is our redemption; and we see the light of the knowledge of the glory of God in His face.

*　　*　　*

But if He did *not* rise from the dead all that is unique and authoritative about Him at once disappears. If He died as all men die, and did not rise again, if His body mouldered into dust long ago in an unknown grave, He is no more than we are, and He has no right to command us or to counsel us. If His epitaph is dust to dust, He is but one of millions of men who have lived and died.

If He rose from the dead, He triumphed over all the powers of death and hell. He is the Lord of life. But if He did not rise from the dead, that means that our hope and our only hope is lost for ever, for all our aspirations and all our achievements have gone, and will go, down the same way to dusty death.

*　　*　　*

This is not merely a loss to the believer; it is a loss to all humanity, for all our human hopes are really bound up with Christ and His Resurrection. As Walt Whitman wrote, in his grotesque way: 'If worms and rats end us, then Alarum! we are betrayed!' That is literally true, for all that is best in humanity and in the universe around us leads us to a belief in the immortal life, and if that is a delusion it means the whole of existence is fundamentally treacherous. Life is a swindle: we have all been cheated if there is no life beyond the grave.

Everything in our human life here depends for its real worth upon a quality of enduring and eternal existence. All morality means that what we do matters. All religion means that what we are matters—not for a day or two but everlastingly. Take away that lasting quality from human life or human experience and the worth goes out of everything. There is nothing that matters much; there is nothing that is worth while; if all that life means is a little stir in the dust, a few fleeting years here on this earth, and then all will be as if it had never been at all.

* * *

That is the only outlook if Christ did not rise from the dead, for all the hope of immortality (and indeed all the other hopes of men) are embodied in Him. All those hopes died with Him and have risen again with Him, and if He did not rise from the dead, both He and they are dead for ever.

That is the gloomy and desperate alternative, and we ought to face it frankly. This is what the Apostle Paul does. He asks: 'But if Christ is not risen'—what? And he answers honestly: 'Our preaching is vain, your faith is vain: ye are yet in your sins: those who have fallen asleep in Christ have perished.' All that is left is a savage despair: 'Let us eat and drink, for tomorrow we die!' That is what it comes to. Our life is, as the poet says:

A life of nothings, nothing worth,
From that first nothing ere our birth,
To that last nothing under earth.

* * *

We never have a worthy conception of what our Lord is and what He has done until we realize the absolutely universal range of what He was and what He did. There is a very striking phrase in Goethe's *Faust* where the great German poet makes Mephistopheles, the spirit of evil, say:

Ich bin der Geist der stets verneint

—I am the spirit that evermore denies. Our Lord is the spirit that evermore affirms. The religion of Christ denies nothing but what is evil. Everything else in this wonderful world, everything else in the experience of humanity, Christ affirms at its best. There is nothing narrowing about the spirit of Christianity. It is all expansive, all affirmative, all positive. The Apostle Paul knew this, and one of his great sayings is: 'In Him is the yea; wherefore also through Him is the Amen, unto the glory of God through us.'

It is true that there is an element of restriction in practical religion, but on a close examination it will always be found that any element of restraint is always in the interest of a larger truth and a larger life. It is not restraint for its own sake, but restraint for the sake of a greater good.

* * *

Yes, that is what is inevitably involved in the Resurrection of our Lord. It is not alone the validity of His own life, so to speak, but the worth and significance and the validity of all human life, for the reality and worth of human life depend upon the possession of an eternal quality, a quality that issues from God, that was before the elements and owes no homage to the sun.

If what I am and what I do matters everlastingly, and matters in the sight of God, then my life is well worth living. It is not a tale told by an idiot, full of sound and fury, signifying nothing. It is a life given to me by God, a life to be lived to His glory, a life which may know a love which passes knowledge, and a peace that passes understanding, a life which becomes life eternal. If life means that, I am glad to be alive, and I am glad to spend myself in the service of God and of goodness: it is worth while, and unspeakably worth while.

But if our Lord did not rise again, if He is not alive now, and at the right hand of God, if He died upon the Cross and that was the end of Him, then what you and I are, and what we do, does not matter much, for we and all the world and all things go down into nothingness.

* * *

It is strange how fortuitous the religious view of many can be. Often we do not see the bearing of our faith upon our own life and the lives of those we know and love; often we do not see the bearing of it upon the life of all humanity, upon the life of the cosmos. Our Lord is the cosmic Christ: in Him all things consist. The fate of the world and the fate of all things in it are finally bound up with Him.

* * *

That strange American genius, Edgar Allan Poe, has a terrible poem in which he imagines the end of the world as the last act of a stupendous drama, acted before an audience of seraphs. The climax comes when a crawling shape comes on the stage and devours the human actors, and

the angels, all pallid and wan,
Uprising, unveiling, affirm
That the play is the tragedy, 'Man',
And its hero the Conqueror Worm.

That is the real issue at Easter. Is the final victory with Christ or with the Worm? with life and love, or with death and corruption?

* * *

Let us rejoice with unspeakable joy, because we know that Jesus the Conqueror reigns, and we reign with Him. Thanks be to God who giveth us the victory through our Lord Jesus Christ! Alleluia! Christ is risen! He is risen indeed! Alleluia!